Oliver Prescott Hiller

A chapter on slavery

Presenting a sketch of its origin and history, with the reasons for its permission, and the probable manner of its removal

Oliver Prescott Hiller

A chapter on slavery

Presenting a sketch of its origin and history, with the reasons for its permission, and the probable manner of its removal

ISBN/EAN: 9783744738668

Printed in Europe, USA, Canada, Australia, Japan

Cover: Foto ©Suzi / pixelio.de

More available books at **www.hansebooks.com**

A CHAPTER ON SLAVERY:

PRESENTING

A SKETCH OF ITS ORIGIN AND HISTORY,

WITH THE

REASONS FOR ITS PERMISSION,

AND

THE PROBABLE MANNER OF ITS REMOVAL.

BY THE

REV. O. PRESCOTT HILLER,
AUTHOR OF "GOD MANIFEST," "PRACTICAL SERMONS," ETC.

LONDON:
HODSON & SON, 22, PORTUGAL STREET.
NEW YORK: MASON, BROTHERS, 587, MERCER STREET.
BOSTON: OTIS CLAPP, 3, BEACON STREET.
1860.

PREFACE.

THIS little work is entitled *A Chapter on Slavery*, because it was originally written as a Chapter of the author's lately published work, *God Manifest*. The object of that work was to set forth the goodness and wisdom of God, as manifested in his works and Word, and also to explain the reasons for the permission of evil in the world. In elucidating the latter subject, various evils, moral, physical, and social, were cited as examples, and the causes of their permission sought to be made plain. *Slavery* was one of the evils intended to be dwelt upon, and its origin shown, together with the reasons for its temporary permission, under Divine Providence, and the probable mode of its future removal. But the Chapter, when written out, being found to be quite disproportionate, in length, to its proper place in a work of that general character, it was thought best to omit it from that work, and publish it in a separate form. Hence the present publication.

In treating this interesting subject, the author has striven to speak in a calm and dispassionate manner,—the only way, indeed, in which a matter involving such great and varied interests ought to be spoken of. He has endeavored to look at it not merely from a civil and a moral point of view, but also from a spiritual one —from which it has not, perhaps, been sufficiently contemplated. He has sought to show the workings of a Divine Providence in the permission of negro slavery, the probable object of that permission, and the means already in operation by which the same Providence designs to bring it gradually to an end. He has sought to make the reflecting, and particularly the religious, portion of the community who are interested in this subject, feel and realize—what in principle they must know to be true—that this great concern, affecting, as it does, the welfare of so many millions of human beings, has not been abandoned by an over-ruling Providence, and is by no means disregarded by a God of goodness—as some in their haste and passion seem to think—but that He is working for it quietly, but effectively, and that in due time He will show His hand, and bring forth the desired result.

Finally, the writer has endeavored, in discussing this somewhat exciting subject, to do justice to all parties concerned: to exonerate the Americans, his countrymen, so far as he thinks they deserve exoneration; to lay upon the European originators of American slavery their due share of the blame; but, especially, to show that in Africa itself is to be sought the true fountain and source of the slavery of Africans in the New World: thus, that negro slavery is but another instance of evil and moral degradation punishing itself. Yet, in conclusion, looking rather to the future than to the present or the past, he has endeavored to hold out the hope of a final deliverance from this evil, and to show the means by which he believes that deliverance is ultimately to be accomplished.

September 24, 1860.

CONTENTS.

SECTION I.
GENERAL VIEW OF THE SUBJECT—SLAVERY IN ANCIENT TIMES—IN THE MIDDLE AGES, ... 1

SECTION II.
SLAVERY IN RUSSIA, ... 14

SECTION III.
SLAVERY IN AFRICA, ... 31

SECTION IV.
THE REPUBLIC OF LIBERIA, ... 61

SECTION V.
DISTINCT CHARACTER OF THE COLORED RACE—WHY THE AFRICAN SLAVE TRADE HAS BEEN PERMITTED—EMIGRATION OF THE FREE BLACKS TO LIBERIA, . . . 95

SECTION VI.
SLAVERY IN AMERICA—ITS ORIGIN—AND THE PROBABLE MANNER OF ITS REMOVAL, ... 120

A CHAPTER ON SLAVERY.

SECTION I.

GENERAL VIEW OF THE SUBJECT—SLAVERY IN ANCIENT TIMES—IN THE MIDDLE AGES.

It may seem, to the casual observer, strange and unaccountable, that, if there be a great and overruling Providence, a wise and good Being, the Creator and Father of all, He should suffer any of His intelligent creatures—still more, such numbers of them—to be held in bondage, in absolute subjection to the will and caprice of their fellow-men. He wonders that the God above looks on and suffers such wrongs; he wonders that He does not send down His lightning-bolts, and break their chains in an instant. But one who thinks more deeply will take a wider and a wiser view of the subject. Reflecting on the present nature of man, he perceives that slavery is but one of the great black branches, springing from the poisonous root of *evil* in the human heart;—that it is one of the direct and natural consequences of man's fall.

The essential principle of evil is *self-love*—a preference of self to others; as the essential principle of goodness is the *love of others* in an equal degree with, or in preference to, ourselves. The latter is the Divine character, for "God is Love;" it is the character of Him who came to "give His life a ransom for many." So it is of all who become conformed to His image and likeness. It is the character of angels: "Are they not all," says the Apostle, "ministering spirits, sent forth to minister for them who shall be heirs of salvation?"* It is the delight of angelic beings to bless and to do good to each other and to man. So, among men, disinterested benevolence, the love of others, an unselfish devotion to the good and happiness of one's fellow-men,—when united to and founded upon a love and worship of the Lord—is acknowledged to be the very test of essential goodness of heart. But, on the other hand, self-love or selfishness, an indifference to the comfort and welfare of one's fellow-men, and a consequent disregard of their rights and interests in comparison with one's own,—is felt by all to be the essential and moving principle of evil in the human heart. All the various forms of evil seen in the world are, indeed, but sprouts from this germ. Pride, contempt, hate, avarice, envy, anger and fury against others, proceeding even to the extent of murder,—all these are direct derivatives from a single source, *Self-love*.

Now, one of the most common forms in which this essential principle of evil appears, is that of the love of dominion,—the disposition to *rule over others*. Such a disposition, it is plain, is the direct and natural offspring of self-love. If a man prefer himself to others, and consequently is seeking to secure his own

* Hebrews i. 14.

interests and effect his own objects, without regard to the welfare and happiness of others, he will naturally seek to bring them into subjection to himself, to make them his instruments, and to cause them to serve him in every way in his power. If he be a ruler, or in public life, he will tyrannize over his countrymen. If in private life, he will show the same selfish disposition in all his business transactions: he will cunningly seek to turn the labors of others to his own advantage; he will get from others all he can, and give as little as possible in return. If an employer, he will task his men to the utmost, reckless of their health or comfort, and this, too, at the lowest wages possible; or if an employé, he will get from his master all in his power, and render as little honest return of labor as he can. For, the same selfish principle works in both ways: the servant seeks to rule the master, as well as the master the servant. This truth no one will misunderstand; for, alas! we may see this demon at work everywhere about us in society, and every hour in the day: we may find it in our own hearts, too, if we search for it. For, this evil passion, the love of rule, the disposition to subject others to ourselves, is as universal as self-love; and self-love, in this fallen day, is born in every heart. Hence it is so common, that many hardly conceive it to be evil at all; and some even hold it to be a virtue,—little thinking that it is in man's heart the essential germ of hell: it is Satan himself that says (as represented by the poet),

"Better to rule in hell, than serve in heaven."

Now, slavery is nothing more than one form of the love of rule, existing in manifest exercise, and established in power. It is simply the result of circumstances so operating as to permit that natural love of rule, which exists in every unregenerate heart, to carry itself into act and unrestrained indulgence. Hence we may expect to find the custom of slavery existing from very ancient times. For as soon as evil was born in the human heart, that self-love, which is its essential principle, would begin to show itself in the desire to bring others into subjection and servitude. The father would tyrannize over his children, the older brother over the younger ones, the stronger over the weaker. The patriarch would seek to exercise absolute sway over his family and dependents; and in the contests which self-love would soon cause to arise between one shepherd and another, captives would be taken, who would at once be made slaves,—that is, would be compelled to remain in subjection to their conqueror, and labor for his comfort and at his pleasure. Wherever might is made the only law of right, a state of slavery at once ensues. Then, as communities became enlarged, and small kingdoms established, the king or ruler would be the master of his subjects, holding their property and lives at his disposal. Such, we know, is the state of nearly all Oriental countries to this day: the inhabitants are all in a manner slaves,—the king is their general master. The example set by the superior would be followed by inferiors: each subject would, in his turn, have slaves, as many as he was able to procure and support. These would be captives taken in war, or sometimes insolvent debtors, or, in fine, any persons whom superior wealth or power could bring into one's possession. Thus slavery, beginning in early times, would become at length a general and almost universal institution.

This view we find borne out by all historical testimony. "Slavery and the slave-trade," says an eminent historian, "are older than the records of human society. They are found to have existed wherever the savage hunter began to assume the habits of pastoral or agricultural life; and with the exception of Australasia, they have extended to every portion of the globe. They pervaded every nation of civilized antiquity. The earliest glimpses of Egyptian history exhibit pictures of bondage; the oldest monuments of human labor on the Egyptian soil are evidently the results of slave-labor. The founder of the Jewish nation was a slave-holder and a purchaser of slaves. Every patriarch was lord in his own household. The Hebrews, when they burst the bonds of their own thraldom, carried with them beyond the desert the institution of slavery. Slavery planted itself even in the Promised Land. The Hebrew father might doom his daughter to bondage; the wife and children and posterity of the emancipated slave remained the property of the master and his heirs. It is even probable, that, at a later period, a man's family might be sold for the payment of his debts. The countries that bordered on Palestine were equally familiar with domestic servitude; and, like Babylon, Tyre also, the oldest and most famous commercial city of Phœnicia, was a market for the 'persons of men.' The Scythians of the desert had already established slavery throughout the plains and forests of the unknown North.

"Old as are the traditions of Greece, the existence

of slavery is still older. The wrath of Achilles grew out of the quarrel for a slave; the Grecian dames had crowds of servile attendants; the heroes before Troy made incursions into the neighboring villages and towns, to enslave the inhabitants. Greek pirates, roving, like the corsairs of Barbary, in quest of men, laid the foundations of Greek commerce; each commercial town was a slave-mart; and every cottage near the sea-side was in danger from the kidnapper. Greeks enslaved each other. The Grecian city, that made war on its neighbor city, exulted in its captives as a source of profit; the hero of Macedon sold men of his own kindred and language into hopeless slavery. The idea of universal free labor had not been generated. Aristotle had written that all mankind were brothers; yet the thought of equal enfranchisement never presented itself to his sagacious understanding. In every Grecian republic slavery was an indispensable element.

"The wide diffusion of bondage throughout the dominions of Rome, and the extreme severities of the Roman law towards the slave, contributed to hasten the fall of the Roman commonwealth. The power of the father to sell his children, of the creditor to sell his insolvent debtor, of the warrior to sell his captive, carried the influence of the institution into the bosom of every Roman family, into the conditions of every contract, into the heart of every unhappy land that was invaded by the Roman eagle. The slave-markets of Rome were filled with men of every complexion and of every clime.

"When the freedom of savage life succeeded in

establishing its power on the ruins of the Roman empire, the great swarms of Roman slaves began to disappear; but the middle age witnessed rather a change in the channels of the slave-trade, than a diminution of its evils. The pirate, and the kidnapper, and the conqueror, still continued their pursuits. The Saxon race carried the most repulsive forms of slavery to England, where not half the population could assert a right to freedom, and where the price of a man was but four times the price of an ox. The importation of foreign slaves was freely tolerated; in defiance of severe penalties, the Saxons sold their own kindred into slavery on the Continent; nor could the traffic be checked, till religion, pleading the cause of humanity, made its appeal to conscience. Even after the Conquest, slaves were exported from England to Ireland, till the reign of Henry II., when a national synod of the Irish,—to remove the pretext for an invasion,—decreed the emancipation of all English slaves in the island.

"The German nations made the shores of the Baltic the scenes of the same desolating traffic; and the Dnieper formed the highway on which Russian merchants conveyed to Constantinople the slaves that had been purchased in the markets of Russia. The wretched often submitted to bondage, as the bitter but only refuge from absolute want. But it was the long wars between the German and Slavonic tribes, which imparted to the slave-trade its greatest activity, and filled France and the neighboring states with such numbers of victims that they gave the name of the *Slavonic* nation to servitude itself; and every country of western Europe still preserves in its language the record of the barbarous traffic in '*Slaves*.'" *

From the account here given we may see how widespread, both in ancient and in modern times, has been the existence of slavery. And the reason already assigned sufficiently explains a fact which would seem otherwise so strange, viz., that slavery, or the disposition to enslave one's fellow-men, springs directly and naturally from the *love of rule*, which evil passion is the immediate offspring of that *self-love* which is the essential principle of evil. Hence we see that slavery has been almost as extensive and as universal as evil itself. Here, then, we have the true answer to the question, "Why does God not at once send down His thunderbolts and break all slave-chains at a blow?— why does He permit such wrongs?" He does not destroy it for the same reason that He does not destroy any other evil and all evils: He permits it for the same reason that He permits the existence of evil at all in the world. The essential reason for the permission of any particular evil is to prevent a greater; and the reason for the permission of sin itself, is because it was the only alternative to the destruction of man's mental liberty, and the consequent non-existence of any rational and intelligent creatures in the universe. The possession of reason or rationality, together with mental liberty, is essential to man as man: without it he would be a stock or a statue, or but as one of the lower animals,—either inanimate or irrational. But rationality and liberty imply the power of thought and of choice—the power to turn to this side or that, to

* *Bancroft's History of the United States*, vol. i., chap. v.

look upward or downward, to turn *to* God or *from* God. Turning from God to self, and resting in and depending upon self, at length begat self-dependence, self-love, sin. Thus the possession of reason and mental liberty necessarily implied the *possibility* of sin or evil. God permitted this possibility to go into actuality,—or in other words, permitted evil, because, as just shown, it could not be prevented without destroying reason and liberty, thus destroying the essential human constitution—humanity itself. And He saw it to be better that there should be some bad humanity, than no humanity at all. He saw it to be better that there should be some evil in the world, than no good; some suffering, than no happiness; better, even, that there should be a hell, than no heaven. For what, after all, is that which is called hell, in its essence? It is simply a perverted mental state, into which the evil have themselves brought themselves. Abusing that mental liberty which is given to every man, they have chosen a perverse course, and adhered to it till it has at length become fixed with them: in the solemn words of Scripture, they have "chosen death rather than life."* But shall the millions, and millions, and millions more, of the good, who have lived, and have yet to live in the lapse of coming ages, be deprived of that joyous inheritance which the good Creator has provided for all who will accept of it—simply because some do not choose to have it? Surely, not. The whole scheme of existence, in a word, is this: God, in His infinite love, creates myriads and millions of beings, to the end that He may bless them and make them

* Jeremiah viii. 3.

happy forever. But, in order that they may be gifted with the highest kind of blessing and happiness,—a happiness akin to His own Divine joy,—they must be rational and intelligent creatures, formed, thus, after His own image and likeness. Such a high nature implies mental liberty. Now, those who will not abuse this liberty, but keep themselves in the original and healthful order in which they were created, are capable of receiving the eternal happiness which the good Creator designed for them; but those who, abusing their liberty, pervert and disorder their moral natures, render themselves incapable of receiving it, and, on the contrary, bring themselves into a state of unhappiness. This latter state is what is called hell—the former, heaven.

Such, then, we see, is the reason for the permission of evil in general. Slavery, as one of the natural fruits of evil—the natural offspring of man's selfishness and sin—was necessarily permitted also: the tree must bring forth its own fruit.

For that social disease, however, the Savior, when he came into the world, brought a remedy, which, in his Divine wisdom, he knew would be gradually but certainly effectual. He did not violently attack the institution of slavery, though existing all around him, and indeed throughout the known world, at that time; he made no open assault upon it, for "he knew what was in man,"—he knew better how to reach the human heart. He laid down a great law, the law of love: "Whatsoever ye would that men should do to you, do ye even so to them." As this seed of heavenly truth became sown, and took root in the human heart, and expanded and grew, he knew that it would gradually up-root and cast out the weeds—he knew that selfish and evil passions could not endure its celestial atmosphere, and that the poisonous fruits and flowers of those Upas trees would one by one wither and drop off. This would be the case, both individually and nationally. As the individual received into his mind the law of love, and, aided by the Divine strength, strove to bring that law into action, and thus sought to do to others as he would wish others to do to him,— he could not wilfully hold his fellow-man in slavish bondage, feast indolently on the fruits of another's toil, and deprive his brother of that liberty which was to himself so dear: the law of love forbade it. Again, as a nation, or political society (which is, in fact, but an aggregate of individuals), became impressed with the same thought, and imbued with the same spirit, it would not willingly suffer any institution or order of things to exist within its bosom, which stood opposed to that Divine principle. It would freely and of its own accord, and without any need of violence or assault from without, throw out from its midst those bonds, which, while they enchained others, were also fetters on itself, and clogs to its own prosperity and peace. It would do so, however, not merely from policy or from selfish calculation of effects and consequences, but from high principle. The national heart, impressed with the great law, "love thy neighbor as thyself," could not bear to see men within its borders oppressed and trodden down under the feet of fellow-men,—slaves to another's will, toiling day and night for another's advantage. The injustice of such a state of things would

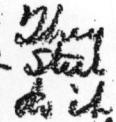

strike them forcibly: the public conscience, enlightened from above, could not endure this wrong, and they would meet together and resolve, with one heart and one voice, to put an end to it. And, in that State or Nation, slavery would cease. And thus would the ball of light and heavenly fire roll on from nation to nation, dissipating the dark stains of slavery as it went, till at length the whole earth would be purified; and then would this orb of ours go glittering on its way through the heavens, worthy to be looked upon by angels' eyes.

This effect the All-Wise Savior foresaw when he announced that law of love: "A new commandment give I unto you,—that ye love one another." And this result, though not yet complete, is, nevertheless, in great part accomplished. Most of Europe is now enfranchised. Greece, which, at the time our Lord was upon earth, was full of slaves, has now not one. Rome, whose "slave-markets," as shown in the testimony before adduced, "were filled with men of every complexion and every clime," has no slave-market now. Other forms of oppression, indeed, yet exist there; but that of domestic servitude, at least, is wanting. Most of the other nations of Europe — Northern Italy, France, Germany, England, which during the middle ages, all contained hordes of bondmen—are now delivered from this evil and purged from this stain. And this is all the direct result of the influence of Christianity, working quietly but deeply in the heart of society; accomplishing its great purposes without violence or noise or rude attack; acting, not as the storm but as the sunshine,—melting the frosty bonds by the power of love; and by the warmth of genial charity, causing man to cast from him the cloak of selfishness, which the blasts of abuse would have only made him wrap more closely about him. Enfranchisement, effected in this gentle and gradual manner, is, like mercy,

" Twice blessed;
It blesseth him that gives and him that takes."

And this, we are persuaded, is the only way it ever has been or can be accomplished, to the lasting good and advantage of both or either of the parties concerned, the master or the slave.

SECTION II.

SLAVERY IN RUSSIA.

Russia now remains, we believe, the only nation of Europe that still contains within its borders large numbers of hereditary bondmen. The people, from whom the term *Slave* was originally derived—the *Slavonian* or *Slavonic* race—is still the one, and the only remaining one in Europe, among whom exists the condition of slavery. The number of people there held in bondage is indeed immense and startling to hear. In Russia (including Poland) there are upwards of *forty millions* of slaves,—more than ten times the number of those in the United States of America. It is common, indeed, to call these people *serfs;* but that is only a different term for the same thing—the word *serf* (from the Latin *servus*) signifying a *slave.* As the term *serf*, however, conveys no very distinct idea to the English mind, we prefer to use one that is clearly defined—viz., *slaves;* for they are truly slaves. "Slavery," as defined by Paley, "is the obligation to labor for the benefit of the master, without the contract or consent of the servant:" and such, certainly, is the condition of these 40,000,000 of persons. They toil for a master without compensation; they are his property, and are called *things* rather than persons; they are bought and sold—usually, though not always, with the land—their price varying from 700 to 2,000 roubles each; they are subject to the master's absolute will, and may be punished by the lash or in any other manner the master may choose, and to any extent, saving life and limb. They cannot marry but at his pleasure or with his consent. If they run away, they may be pursued and brought back; or if found at any time, even though it be ten years after, they must be returned to the owner.* A "fugitive-slave law" is there in full force; and indeed what else is to be expected, wherever slavery exists at all? If a slave could obtain his freedom, simply by becoming a *fugitive*, that is, by running away, slavery, of course, could not long continue, whether in Russia or elsewhere. The Russian government, also, interdicts every kind of instruction to the serfs: ignorance is the necessary guard of slavery. Moreover, it is very difficult for the serfs even to purchase their freedom—as the pride of the nobles renders them oftentimes unwilling to sell at any price. There are, indeed, some ameliorating circumstances attending Russian servitude. It is, for instance, forbidden by the Russian law, to announce in the public papers any sale of serfs without lands, or to proceed publicly to such sales at fairs or markets. Proprietors, moreover, cannot divide families, separating husband from wife, or unmarried children from their parents.† But notwithstanding these modifications,

* See "*Russia under Nicholas*," by Ivan Golovine, vol. ii., ch. i.
† Ibid.

the condition of this immense and unfortunate class is bad enough.*

The abject misery of a great part of her inhabitants was probably a chief cause of the downfall of Poland. It was called a Republic, because the monarchy was elective: but what sort of a republic was that, in which but 100,000 of the citizens were freemen, and the remaining *eleven millions,* serfs or slaves—whose only spur to industry was the master's lash? We deplore the misfortunes of that oppressed country, and are apt to wonder that an overruling Providence should permit such wrong. But if we look more deeply into the state of the case, we shall find that in this as in most other instances, it is man's own evils that bring upon him what are called misfortunes. The partition of Poland could never have taken place had it been united within itself, and had its people been bound together by the firm bands of truth and justice. Ninety-nine hundredths of the people were bondmen, with no voice whatever in the government, and with

* Alexander Herzen, a Russian, writing in one of the London journals, in November, 1853, says: "It is an established and constant practice to *sell* serfs, if not separately, at least by family.—The lord is under no obligation to his servants beyond supplying them with just enough food and clothing to prevent their perishing with hunger and cold.—The lord has the right to have them flogged, only not to death." The writer adds, somewhat tartly: "Shall these monstrosities continue, without an incessant, universal protest? The mask must be torn from these *Slaveholders of the North,* who go lounging over Europe, mingling with your affairs, assuming the rank of civilized beings,—nay, of liberal-minded men, who read 'Uncle Tom's Cabin' with horror, and shudder when they read of sellers of *black* flesh. Why, these same brilliant spies of the *salons* are the very ones who on their return to their domains rob, flog, sell the *white* slave, and are served at table by their living property."

no rights to defend. "The Polish serf," says a writer, "drowned in brandy all activity of mind, for his motto was,—'Only what I drink is mine.' At the same time the masters were divided among themselves, engaged in perpetual dissensions, and living in luxury and corruption. The throne was sold to the highest bidder. In its moral tone, too, which aimed at uniting French wit and frivolousness with excess and rudeness, Poland had gone back many steps towards the times of violence. Religious animosities, also, raged through the country. Encroachments were made by the Catholics on the constitutional rights of the Dissidents, that is, the Protestants and Greek Church; and this destruction of religious freedom was a main cause of the civil war which plunged Poland into the wildest disorder, and accelerated the ruin of the state. Russia embraced the cause of the Dissidents; foreign troops laid waste the country; and the lawless conduct of some of the Polish party chiefs excited among the neighboring Powers such a contempt of the natural rights of the Poles, that, to use the expression of Catherine, they deemed Poland a country in which it was 'only necessary to stoop to pick up something.'"* Such was the distracted state of the nation when the infamous plan of partition was formed by the three neighboring Powers; and this, their own death-warrant, was, under Russian compulsion, signed by the Polish Diet itself. Could anything have brought the nation to such ignominy, but their own internal weakness, the result of moral unworthiness? No excuse whatever, indeed, is this for the infamous conduct of the oppressors and partitioners of

* *Encyclopædia Americana*, article "Poland."

c

Poland: the weakness or debased condition of his victim is no justification of the robber. But a true view of the case is highly important, as the means of justifying or explaining to our minds the dispensations or permissions of Divine Providence, which could allow such an unhappy result to be brought about. The original and essential cause, we see, of Poland's destruction, was her own internal disorder. Thus it is, that moral evil, whether in individuals or in nations, ever leads to physical suffering.

Russia, too, has herself suffered, and must continue to suffer—internally, at least, if not from any foreign aggression—in consequence of so many of her people being held in bondage. A census of Russia, published about the year 1848, rates the whole population at fifty-three millions, five hundred thousand souls; of which number only eleven millions and a half are free persons—the remaining forty-two millions being serfs or slaves. Of the latter, fifteen millions belong to the crown,* and twenty-seven millions to private individuals. Thus, in Russia, only one man in five is free: four-fifths of the inhabitants are slaves.† What widespread suffering must be the consequence of such a state of things! Slaves to the absolute will of masters, who are, many of them, in a semi-barbarous state, in a severe climate, too, like that of Russia, and with the soil but half-cultivated—what sufferings must the serfs often endure from cold and want, as well as from the

---

* It thus appears that the Emperor of Russia is by far the greatest slaveholder in the world, his own serfs numbering nearly five times all the slaves in the United States.

† Thompson's *Life in Russia*, Letter xv.

cruelty of their masters! "These feudal lords," says Mr. Thompson,* "are of extravagant and profligate habits, and occasionally harass their serfs with the most grinding oppression and extortion, while their neglect or inability to provide the stores and magazines directed by the government, reduce their serfs, in unpropitious seasons, to want and the most horrible sufferings from famine. This occurred to a frightful extent in 1840, in the governments of Toula, Riazan, and Kalouga, when the people were driven for subsistence to the bark of trees. The summer of 1839 was so excessively hot, that the parched land yielded no produce, and that of 1840 was so cold and wet, that the crops entirely failed. The consequence was, that the most dreadful distress prevailed, and thousands perished from starvation." Insurrections, also, have occasionally occurred, rivaling the horrors of St. Domingo. "Intoxicated with the belief," says the same writer, "that they might emancipate themselves, they organized a powerful conspiracy; and arming themselves, desolated the country around them with fire and sword, perpetrating horrors not to be exceeded by the sanguinary scenes of St. Domingo, or the worst days of the French Revolution. It is stated that they cut off the legs and arms of their victims, beating them to death with the mutilated members, and stifling their dreadful cries by thrusting the mangled feet into their mouths."† Such is the terrible retaliation that sometimes follows a long course of oppression and wrong.

To show the summary and arbitrary manner in

* *Life in Russia*, Letter viii. † Ibid.

which the house-serfs are punished for occasional carelessness or neglect, the following circumstance is related by the author already quoted:—"Attached to every house is a man called a *dvornik* or yard-man, whose duty it is to keep the street clean in front of his master's house, to scrape the snow from off the pavement, and to strew it with sand, to prevent accidents to foot passengers. The Emperor, in walking the street, slipped and fell. He took down the name of the house he was passing, and going straight to the nearest police-station, directed the dvornik of that house to be seized and flogged. Short was the shrift allowed the offender; a Persian bastinado would not have been more prompt. Surrounded by all the dvorniks of the neighborhood, collected for the purpose of being edified by the example, stood the unfortunate culprit, in the presence of the whole staff of the police of the district. In the centre of the yard lay a form and two bundles of birchen rods, and all was anxious expectation. At a signal, every head was uncovered, in deference, probably, to the authority represented by the punishment; and though the thermometer was at ten degrees below freezing-point, the offender was seized, stripped, and laid flat on the bench. One man sat on his legs, another held his arms crossed beneath the bench; while, on each side of him, with a bundle of rods under their arms, stood two others, cutting away alternately at him, and exchanging the rods as often as they got dull, until the whole were expended."*
"Such," says the writer, "is the paternal discipline" of the Russian autocrat. How would this Imperial

* *Thompson*, Letter iii.

master* feel, if the slight lapses from duty, of which he, as every man, before God is guilty, were as severely visited?

This, however, was a light punishment, compared with the terrible one of the *knout*, to which the Russian slaves who are guilty of weightier offences, such as crimes, are subjected. One hundred to one hundred and twenty strokes of this terrible instrument are considered equivalent to death! indeed, it is often more dreaded than death itself, so that a criminal has been known to bribe the executioner to kill him instead. Howard, the philanthropist, while in Russia, witnessed this painful punishment, and thus describes it:—"The knout-whip is fixed to a wooden handle, a foot long, and consists of several thongs about two feet in length, twisted together; to the end of which is fastened a single tough thong of a foot and a half, and capable of being changed by the executioner, when too much softened by the blood of the criminal. I saw two criminals," he says, "a man and a woman, suffer the punishment of the knout. They were conducted from prison by about fifteen hussars and ten soldiers. When they arrived at the place of punishment, the hussars formed themselves into a ring round the whipping-post—the drum beat a minute or two—and then some prayers were read, the populace taking off their hats. The woman was taken first; and after being roughly stripped to the waist, her hands and feet were bound with cords to a post made for the purpose, a man standing before the post, and holding the cords

---

* The Emperor, here referred to, was not the present Emperor, but Nicholas.

to keep them tight. A servant attended the executioner, and both were stout men. The servant first marked his ground and struck the woman five times on the back. Every stroke seemed to penetrate deep into her flesh. But his master thinking him too gentle, pushed him aside, took his place, and gave all the remaining strokes himself, which were evidently more severe. The woman received twenty-five and the man sixty. I pressed through the hussars, and counted the number as they were chalked on a board: both seemed but just alive, especially the man, who yet had strength enough to receive a small donation, with some signs of gratitude. They were conducted back to prison in a little waggon. I afterwards saw the woman in a very weak condition, but could not find the man any more."*

Suspecting that this punishment frequently occasioned the death of the sufferer, and that it was sometimes intended to produce this effect, Howard visited the executioner, and assuming an air of authority, demanded truthful replies to certain interrogations: "Can you inflict the *knout* in such a manner as to occasion death in a short time?"—"I can," was the reply. "In how short a time?"—"In a day or two." "Have you ever so inflicted it?"—"Yes! the last man who was punished by my hands with the *knout*, died of the punishment!" "In what manner do you thus render it mortal?"—"By one or more strokes on the sides, which carry off large pieces of flesh!!" "Do you receive orders thus to inflict the punishment?"—"I do." †

O cruel man! more savage than the beasts of the forest,—heartless and hard as the stones under his feet!

* Mrs. Farrar's *Life of Howard*, p. 148.   † Ibid., p. 149.

How has he departed from the image of his Maker! how has he turned love into hate! what miseries is he willing to inflict upon his fellow-man!

Mr. Thompson also saw a female slave who, for the crime of arson, had suffered the punishment of the knout, and had recovered from it. "While visiting the prison," says he, "I expressed to Dr. Haas (a philanthropic individual, who has spent his whole life and fortune, after the example of our Howard, in attempting to mitigate the horrors of a prison, and to reform its inmates) a wish to see the effects of the knout. He immediately called out and desired any person who had undergone the punishment, to come forward; when a young woman, of about twenty, presented herself, and, without the slightest hesitation or compunction, bared her back. A twelvemonth had elapsed since the punishment had been inflicted, which, in her case, had been confined to five lashes. The wounds had, of course, long healed, and the skin was perfectly smooth over them; but five red marks of a finger's breadth each, and of considerable length, were indelibly imprinted between her shoulders, as if branded by fire."*

Where is English sympathy? Is there none left for these forty-two millions of enslaved beings, still remaining in Europe,—subject, thus, to the rod, the lash, and the terrible knout,—liable, too, at times, to the horrors of starvation from the recklessness of their haughty masters? Is there no one to write a Russian "Uncle Tom,"† to bring the picture of their wrongs before the world? *Forty-two millions!*—a greater number of white men existing in bondage, this moment, in a single

---

* *Life in Russia,* Letter xix.   † *Uncle Tom's Cabin,* by Mrs. Stowe.

country of Europe, than all the blacks that have been exported from Africa, altogether, in two centuries and a half!* Why is no pity felt for these? Doubtless, simply through ignorance. From the fact of America's speaking the same language, and of there being constant communication between the two countries, everything that is done there is known: while Russia is comparatively locked up, and invisible to the mental view: yet as is the proportion of *forty* millions to *three* millions, so much greater must be the amount of suffering in Russia than in America.

And is not this fact sufficient to show us how narrow are our views of things, how little we know of the real condition of the world, as it appears before God's All-seeing eye, and how little able we are, consequently (when we go beyond our own immediate sphere), to form correct judgments and to direct our efforts aright? Not so with the All-wise Ruler of the world. He looks down upon Russia equally as on America: He hears and sees every lash inflicted on the slave, whether in New Orleans or in Moscow. Yet He is "silent."† But though silent, He is not unobservant or inactive. He does not cry out, when crying out will effect nothing: but in His infinite wisdom, He is silently working to bring about a change and to remove the evil at the soonest possible moment. He is working,‡ but ever wisely, and according to the laws of His own

* The sum total of these has been estimated at from *sixteen to twenty millions.*

† "The gloomiest problem of this mysterious life was constantly before his eyes: souls crushed and ruined,—evil triumphant and God silent."—*Uncle Tom's Cabin*, chap. xxxviii.

‡ "My Father worketh hitherto, and I work."—John v. 17.

Divine order, established for the greatest good of all. These He never violates. And the first of these, as already shown, is the preservation of man's *moral liberty*, the power of moral choice, the liberty of turning to the right or to the left, of looking to God or from God, of taking the upward or the downward path. This first and greatest law of the Divine government He preserves ever inviolate above all others; because, take it away, and man ceases to be man—humanity perishes, and there is left nothing but a universe of inanimate stocks and stones, or only brute and irrational creatures, nothing worthy of God's highest regard, nothing that can return to Him thought for thought, love for love. As shown in the preceding Section, rationality and moral liberty are the distinguishing characteristics of man: if either of them be taken away humanity perishes. It was also shown that the existence of rationality and liberty implies the *possibility* of evil; for evil, as there defined, is in itself simply a perverted and disordered state of mind;—and moral liberty implies the power so to pervert the mind, if one will. This being so, the great purpose of the Divine Being, in His dealings with man, is—while leaving his moral freedom inviolable—still gently to bend him to good. This cannot be done violently and forcibly, for that would be a contradiction: to leave man free and to force him are plainly contradictory. There is no such thing as forcing the will; for the will is the love, and love cannot be forced. This every one sees. It is indeed perfectly possible for the Divine Being to bring forth his thunderbolts—so to speak—and by violence and terror to sweep away slavery or any other evil institution or outward condition of things. But, after all, that would be merely to sweep away the stream, not to purify the fountain: as soon as the storm had passed over, the fountain would begin to pour forth its black waters again. God's wise purpose is not merely to remove the effect, but to change the cause. His great end, it must be remembered, is to regenerate man's heart, not merely to remove temporary suffering. He ever keeps eternity in view—the one end of existence, salvation, heaven. He loves every man, the master as well as the slave, and desires to save all who are willing to be saved. To take away suddenly and violently, therefore, any object of cherished love, even though it be an improper and evil one, would, in many cases, have the effect not of changing the heart or evil desire, but only of maddening it and confirming it more strongly in its evil purpose; the effect of which would be to destroy the soul. Consequently, in His Divine Wisdom, He acts gently, gradually, here a little and there a little, presenting inducements to good on the one hand, gently checking excesses of evil on the other,— introducing higher views, presenting to the mind nobler considerations,—thus gradually working on the spirit, till, at length, the man begins to be ashamed of his own evil course, to repent of it, and voluntarily to give it up and turn to better things. Then has the Divine Wisdom achieved a great triumph. He has not forced the man's will, which would be fruitless or impossible, but He has quietly induced the man to change his own will—voluntarily to turn to the right path: and He has thereby saved a soul.

Such is the manner of the Divine workings. Such is the reason for the permission of slavery and a thousand other evils, whether with individuals or with nations, for years and for ages: and by such a gentle and orderly process, also, will be accomplished their final removal, and the triumph of love, goodness, and happiness throughout the world.

To return. In regard to Russian slavery or serfdom, —it is pleasant to know that some few steps have of late years been taken in the direction of its removal. By a decree of the 2d of April, 1842, the nobles were empowered to emancipate their serfs, on making with them certain agreements. Says a Russian authority already quoted,* "I have hailed this decree as a forerunner of the emancipation of the serfs; in fact, trifling as it may be, still a great deal has been done in broaching the question; and already the fear of seeing the Government one day cut this knot, urges the nobles to prevent its direct interposition, and to remedy the present state of things in one way or another. By the method which the Government has adopted, it has declined the initiative, and thrown the responsibility on the nobles, by opening a clear field for their philanthropy. This was a politic proceeding on its part, and has singularly lightened its task. Having once got so far, no matter whether willingly or unwillingly, it would be pusillanimous to recede; and I seize its decree as a plank of safety. I call upon it, in the name of humanity, to fulfil the engagements which morally it has contracted before the face of the whole world.

* Ivan Golovine, author of *Russia under Nicholas*. 1846.

I think the decree good, because to me it appears moderate, and it respects the pretensions of each, leaving to the nobles, as to the serfs, full latitude to make such agreements as they shall deem advantageous." The author, however, afterwards adds,—" Thus far the results have not corresponded with the hopes entertained. The nobility have not shown that eagerness to enter the track opened for them, which we had a right to expect. Power has not brought the necessary perseverance to bear upon this point, and has incurred the suspicion of timidity or duplicity. The serfs have not sufficient intelligence to frame the conditions of their own enfranchisement, and would be afraid of compromising their future welfare. They distrust the Government more than their masters, and would rather remain serfs, than place themselves in a greater dependence on authority."—"The Russian nobles," he continues, "wish for the emancipation of the serfs, because they are ashamed to pass for slave-traders in the eyes of civilized Europe; because they begin to perceive some profit in emancipation, and to be apprehensive for their own safety, fearing that the serfs may by and by seize that liberty which is now refused them. The Government wishes for it, too, in order to appear well before foreign nations, and to augment its revenues. At this rate, there would be none but the serfs themselves who would not wish their freedom; for to listen to the partizans of the present order of things, their condition is insured at present, but would become quite precarious on the day of their emancipation. If, in fact, the nobles are determined not to part with any of their lands,—in that case, indeed, liberty would be a dangerous weapon in the hands of the serfs." The writer concludes,—"The Government, on the one hand, has not the courage to take a decisive measure, and, on the other, the serfs know not how to stipulate for their interests. The Emperor, yielding to foreign influences, would fain crown himself with an immortal laurel; but he knows not either how to avoid or to meet the dangers which emancipation presents. The half measures which Nicholas has hitherto taken are deficient in energy: it is therefore said that nothing great will be accomplished under this wretched system, and that the heir to the crown will inherit with it all the difficulties which his father was incapable of solving."*

Since the publication of the work from which the above extract is made, Alexander II. has succeeded to the throne, and, as is known, is already taking active measures for the emancipation of the serfs. The grand difficulty which attends emancipation in America— namely, the difference of race and color and the consequent impracticability of amalgamation—has no existence here. The nobles and the serfs are of the same nation and race: the distinction between them is purely artificial; and the law has consequently simply to remove that barrier, and the two classes will easily merge into one. Among the nobles, even now, there are instances of persons, who themselves or whose ancestors were once serfs. In fact, Russia, at the present time, is passing through a transition state similar to that which England and France passed through three or four centuries ago. At that period, as we know, the

* *Russia under Nicholas*, vol. ii., chap. i.

greater part of the inhabitants of those countries were in the condition of serfdom. But with the spread of light, knowledge, and civilization, and above all, of Christianity, the only true liberator,—that condition gradually passed away, and nothing of it now remains. And so, doubtless, will it be with Russia. As the light of truth, with its power, penetrates those hyperborean regions,—as their commerce extends, and communication with the rest of Europe becomes more easy and frequent,—above all, as the warmth of Christian love gradually melts the ice of selfishness in the masters' bosoms,—the bonds of servitude will be relaxed more and more, and finally be dissolved: and the suns of another century will, we trust, shine on Russia, a nation of enlightened freemen.

SECTION III.

SLAVERY IN AFRICA.

WE come now to speak of the slavery of the African race,—a subject which has of late taken so much of the attention of philanthropists. It seems, at first view, one of the most dark and inscrutable permissions of Divine Providence, to suffer the carrying away of thousands and even millions of a particular race of men from their own country, to labor in servitude in other regions of the earth. And some, perhaps, have felt at times disposed to question either the existence or the goodness of an overruling Power, when such a wrong could be permitted to go on so long unchecked. But it would be poor reasoning to conclude that, because our finite and narrow minds cannot at once grasp the purposes of an Omniscient and Infinite Being, therefore such a Being does not exist, when His works all around us testify in the plainest manner to His existence, His wisdom, and His goodness. It would be a far wiser and juster view, to presume that we do not *understand* His designs, than that there are none, or that they are not wise and good. How vast must be His plans, who looks from eternity to eternity, and who is contriving and calculating (to speak according to human language) for ages and ages to come; who patiently waits centuries for His great purposes to be developed, and calls on slumbering futurity to arise and testify to His doings.

It is only by taking a very wide view, that we are enabled to form any conception whatever of the purposes of Divine Providence; and it is scarcely possible to have a distinct understanding of those purposes, until the time arrives when they are beginning to develop themselves in results. From facts which have within the last half-century come to our knowledge, and from events which have been taking place within the last thirty years, we are now able to have some comprehension of the probable designs of Providence in permitting the African slave-trade. The facts to which we refer are the particulars which have been made known to us by recent travelers concerning the interior state of Africa itself. From these we learn, that a great portion of the inhabitants of that country are, and have from the earliest periods been, in a state of slavery amongst themselves. The celebrated traveler, Mungo Park, informs us, that nearly *three-fourths* of all the inhabitants of Africa are in the condition of slaves. And this statement we can the more readily credit, when taken in connection with another, namely, that "hired servants—that is, persons of free condition, working for pay—are unknown" in that country, and that "the labor is universally performed by slaves."*

"A state of subordination," he remarks, in commencing his description of African slavery, "and certain

* Park's *Travels in the Interior of Africa*, chapters i., xxi.

inequalities of rank and condition are inevitable in every stage of civil society; but when this subordination is carried to so great a length as that the persons and services of one part of the community are entirely at the disposal of another part, it may then be denominated a state of slavery: and in this condition of life a great body of the inhabitants of Africa have continued from the most early period of their history,—with this aggravation, that their children are born to no other inheritance." The writer then proceeds to state some particulars concerning the numbers and condition of the slaves as follows :—

"The slaves in Africa are, I suppose, nearly *in the proportion of three to one* to the freemen. They claim no reward for their services except food and clothing, and are treated with kindness or severity according to the good or bad disposition of their masters. Custom, however, has established certain rules with regard to the treatment of slaves, which it is thought dishonorable to violate. Thus, the domestic slaves, or such as are born in a man's house, are treated with more lenity than those which are purchased with money. The authority of the master over the domestic slave extends only to reasonable correction; for the master cannot sell his domestic, without having brought him to a public trial before the chief men of the place. In time of famine, however, the master is permitted to sell one or more of his domestics, to purchase provisions for his family; and in case of the master's insolvency, the domestic slaves are sometimes seized upon by the creditors, and if the master cannot redeem them, they are sold for payment of his debts. These are the only

D

cases that I recollect, in which the domestic slaves are liable to be sold, without any misconduct or demerit of their own. But these restrictions on the power of the master extend not to the case of prisoners taken in war, nor to that of slaves purchased with money. All these unfortunate beings are considered as strangers and foreigners, who have no right to the protection of the law, and may be treated with severity, or sold to a stranger, according to the pleasure of their owners. There are, indeed, *regular markets,* where slaves of this description are bought and sold. And the value of a slave, in the eye of an African purchaser, increases in proportion to his distance from his native kingdom; for when slaves are only a few days' journey from the place of their nativity, they frequently effect their escape; but when one or more kingdoms intervene, escape being more difficult, they are more easily reconciled to their situation. On this account, the unhappy slave is frequently transferred from one dealer to another, until he has lost all hopes of returning to his native kingdom. *The slaves which are purchased by Europeans on the coast are chiefly of this description.* A few of them are collected in the petty wars which take place near the coast, but by far the greater number are brought down in large caravans from the inland countries, of which many are unknown even by name to Europeans.

"The slaves which are thus brought from the interior, may be divided into two distinct classes,—first, such as were slaves from their birth, having been born of enslaved mothers; secondly, such as were born free, but who afterwards by whatever means became slaves.

Those of the first description (born slaves) are by far the most numerous; for prisoners taken in war are generally of this class. The comparatively small proportion of free people to the enslaved, throughout Africa, has been already noticed; and it must be observed, that men of free condition have many advantages over slaves even in war-time. They are in general better armed, and well mounted, and can either fight or escape with some hopes of success; but the slaves, who have only their spears and bows, and great numbers of whom are loaded with baggage, become an easy prey. Thus when Mansong, King of Bambarra, made war upon Kaarta, he took in one day nine hundred prisoners, of whom only seventy were freemen. Again, when a freeman is taken prisoner, his friends will sometimes ransom him, by giving two slaves in exchange; but when a slave is taken, he has no hopes of such redemption. To these disadvantages it is to be added, that the *slatees*, who purchase slaves in the interior countries, and carry them down to the coast for sale, constantly prefer such as have been in that condition of life from their infancy; well knowing that these have been accustomed to hunger and fatigue, and are better able to sustain the hardships of a long and painful journey than freemen. And on reaching the coast, if no opportunity offers of selling them to advantage, they can easily be made to maintain themselves by their labor: neither are they so apt to attempt to make their escape as those who have once tasted the blessings of freedom."

The writer then proceeds to give an account of the manner in which the second class of slaves, or those not born such, become reduced to slavery: this lets us still further into an understanding of the true condition of Africa.

"Slaves of the second description generally become such by one or other of the following causes:—1. Captivity; 2. Famine; 3. Insolvency; 4. Crimes. A freeman may, by the established customs of Africa, become a slave, by being taken in war. War is, of all others, the most productive source, and was probably the origin, of slavery; for when one nation had taken from another a greater number of captives than could be exchanged on equal terms, it is natural to suppose that the conquerors, finding it inconvenient to maintain their prisoners, would compel them to labor,—at first, perhaps, only for their own support, but afterwards to support their masters. Be this as it may, it is a known fact, that prisoners of war in Africa are the slaves of the conquerors; and when the weak or unsuccessful warrior begs for mercy beneath the uplifted spear of his opponent, he gives up at the same time his claim to liberty, and purchases his life at the expense of his freedom.

"In a country divided into a thousand petty states, mostly independent and jealous of each other, where every freeman is accustomed to arms, and fond of military achievements,—where the youth who has practised the bow and spear from his infancy longs for nothing so much as an opportunity to display his valor,—it is natural to imagine that wars frequently originate from very frivolous provocations. When one nation is more powerful than another, a pretext is seldom wanting to commence hostilities. Thus, the war between Kajaaga and Kasson was occasioned by the detention of a fugitive slave;—that between Bambarra and Kaarta by the loss of a few cattle. Other cases of the same nature perpetually occur, in which the folly or mad ambition of their princes, and the zeal of their religious enthusiasts, give full employment to the scythe of desolation.

"The wars of Africa are of two kinds, which are distinguished by different appellations. That species which bears the greatest resemblance to our European contests, is denominated *Killi*, a word signifying 'to call out,' because such wars are openly avowed and previously declared. Wars of this description in Africa commonly terminate, however, in the course of a single campaign. A battle is fought—the vanquished seldom think of rallying again—the whole inhabitants become panic-struck—and the conquerors have only to bind the slaves, and carry off their plunder and their victims. Such of the prisoners as through age or infirmity are unable to endure fatigue, or are found unfit for sale, are considered as useless, and, I have no doubt, are frequently put to death. The same fate commonly awaits a chief, or any other person who has taken a very distinguished part in the war.

"The other species of African warfare is distinguished by the appellation of *Tegria* (plundering or stealing). It arises from a sort of hereditary feud, which the inhabitants of one nation or district bear towards another. No immediate cause of hostility is assigned, or notice of attack given, but the inhabitants of each watch every opportunity to plunder and distress the objects of their animosity by predatory excursions.

These are very common, particularly about the beginning of the dry season, when the labor of the harvest is over, and provisions are plentiful. Schemes of vengeance are then meditated. The chief man surveys the number and activity of his vassals, as they brandish their spears at festivals; and, elated with his own importance, turns his whole thoughts towards revenging some depredation or insult, which either he or his ancestors may have received from a neighboring state. Wars of this description are generally conducted with great secrecy. A few resolute individuals, headed by some person of enterprise and courage, march quietly through the woods, surprise in the night some unprotected village, and carry off the inhabitants and their effects, before their neighbors can come to their assistance. One morning during my stay at Kamalia we were all much alarmed by a party of this kind. The king of Fooladoo's son, with five hundred horsemen, passed secretly through the woods a little to the southward of us, and on the morning following plundered three towns.

"These plundering excursions always produce some speedy retaliation; and when large parties cannot be collected for this purpose, a few friends will combine together, and advance into the enemy's country, with a view to plunder or carry off the inhabitants. A single individual has been known to take his bow and quiver, and proceed in like manner. Such an attempt is doubtless in him an act of rashness; but when it is considered, that in one of these predatory wars he has probably been deprived of his child or his nearest relation, his situation will rather call for pity than censure. The poor sufferer, urged on by the feelings of domestic or paternal attachment, and by the ardor of revenge, conceals himself amongst the bushes, until some young or unarmed person passes by: then, tiger-like, he springs upon his prey, drags his victim into the thicket, and in the night carries him off as his slave."

What a picture of unmitigated barbarism is this! It is surpassed only by the still more ferocious character of the negroes of Dahomey, with whom human skulls are said to constitute the favorite ornament in the construction of palaces and temples; and whose king has the floor of his sleeping-room paved with the skulls, and the ceiling ornamented with the jaw-bones, of the chiefs he has conquered in battle. One of these kings is said to have put to death, at the funeral of his mother, three thousand prisoners, to build a tomb with their skulls.—Park thus continues:

"When a negro has, by means like these, once fallen into the hands of his enemies, he is either retained as the slave of his conqueror, or bartered into a distant kingdom; for an African, when he has once subdued his enemy, will seldom give him an opportunity of lifting up his hand against him at a future period. A conqueror commonly disposes of his captives according to the rank which they held in their native kingdom. Such of the domestic slaves as appear to be of a mild disposition, and particularly the young women, are retained as his own slaves. Others, that display marks of discontent, are disposed of in a distant country; and such of the freemen or slaves as have taken an active part in the war, are either sold to the *slatees* [negro slave-dealers] or are put to death. War, therefore, is certainly the most general and most productive source of slavery.

"The desolations of war, moreover, often produce the second cause of slavery, *famine;* in which case a freeman becomes a slave to avoid a still greater calamity. There are many instances of freemen voluntarily surrendering their liberty to save their lives. During a great scarcity which lasted for three years, in the countries of the Gambia, great numbers of people became slaves in this manner. Dr. Laidley assured me that at that time many freemen came and begged with great earnestness to be put upon his slave-chain, to save them from perishing of hunger. Large families are often exposed to absolute want; and as the parents have almost unlimited authority over their children, it frequently happens, in all parts of Africa, that some of the latter are sold to purchase provisions for the rest of the family. When I was at Jarra, Daman Jumma pointed out to me three young slaves whom he had purchased in this manner.

"The third cause of slavery is *insolvency.* Of all the offences (if insolvency may be so called) to which the laws of Africa have affixed the punishment of slavery, this is the most common. A negro trader commonly contracts debts in some mercantile speculation, either from his neighbors, to purchase such articles as will sell to advantage in a distant market, or from the European traders on the coast—payment to be made in a given time. In both cases the situation of the adventurer is exactly the same. If he succeeds, he may secure an independency: if he is unsuccessful, his person and services are at the disposal of another.

For in Africa, not only the effects of the insolvent, but even the insolvent himself, is sold, to satisfy the lawful demands of his creditors.

"The fourth cause above enumerated is the commission of *crimes* to which the laws of the country have affixed slavery as a punishment.

"When a freeman has become a slave by any one of the causes before mentioned, he generally continues so for life, and his children (if they are born of an enslaved mother) are brought up in the same state of servitude."*

In regard to the treatment of the slaves in Africa, the same author, in addition to the general remarks already quoted, presents some occasional pictures, such as follow (he is describing some of the Moorish tribes on the southern border of the Great Desert):—

"The employment of the women varies according to their degrees of opulence. Queen Fatima and a few others of high rank, like the great ladies in some parts of Europe, pass their time chiefly in conversing with their visitors, performing their devotions, or admiring their charms in a looking-glass. The women of inferior class employ themselves in different domestic duties.

---

* Park's *Travels*, chap. xxii. Another traveler, Bruce, bears striking and painful testimony in regard to the trade in *children* on the northeastern coast of Africa, in the neighborhood of Abyssinia. "This town (Dixan)," says he, "consists of Moors and Christians, and is very well peopled; yet the only trade of either is a very extraordinary one—that of *selling children*. The Christians bring such as they have stolen in Abyssinia to Dixan; and the Moors, receiving them there, carry them to a sure market at Masuah, whence they are sent to Arabia or India." He says, in another place, "About 500 of these unfortunate people are annually exported from Masuah to Arabia; of whom 300 are pagans from the market at Gondar, the other 200 are Christian children kidnapped."—Sir Francis Head's *Life of Bruce*, chap. x., p. 201.

They are vain and talkative; and when anything puts them out of humor, they commonly vent their anger upon their female slaves, over whom they rule with severe and despotic authority,—which leads me to observe, that the condition of these poor captives is deplorably wretched. At day-break they are compelled to fetch water from the wells in large skins; and as soon as they have brought water enough to serve the family for the day, as well as the horses (for the Moors seldom give their horses the trouble of going to the wells), they are then employed in pounding corn and dressing the victuals. This being always done in the open air, the slaves are exposed to the combined heat of the sun, the sand, and the fire. In the intervals, it is their business to sweep the tent, churn the milk, and perform other domestic offices. With all this, they are badly fed, and oftentimes cruelly treated."*

Here is another scene:

"About two o'clock I came to the village of Sooha, and endeavoured to purchase some corn from the *dooty* [chief man of the village], who was sitting by the gate,—but without success. I then requested a little food by way of charity, but was told he had none to spare. Whilst I was examining the countenance of this inhospitable old man, and endeavouring to find out the cause of the sullen discontent which was visible in his eye, he called to a slave who was working in the corn-field at a little distance, and ordered him to bring his hoe along with him. The dooty then told him to dig a hole in the ground,

* Chap. XII.

pointing to a spot at no great distance. The slave with his hoe began to dig a pit in the earth; and the dooty, who appeared to be a man of a very fretful disposition, kept muttering and talking to himself until the pit was almost finished; when he repeatedly pronounced the words *daukatoo* (good for nothing), *jankra lemen* (a real plague),—which expressions I thought could be applied to nobody but myself; and as the pit had very much the appearance of a grave, I thought it prudent to mount my horse, and was about to decamp, when the slave, who had before gone into the village, to my surprise returned with the corpse of a boy about nine or ten years of age, quite naked. The negro carried the body by a leg and an arm, and threw it into the pit with a savage indifference which I had never before seen. As he covered the body with the earth, the dooty often expressed himself *naphula attiniata* (money lost),— whence I concluded that the boy had been one of his slaves."*

Here is a brief description of the pursuit and recovery of a fugitive slave:

"In the afternoon one of his slaves eloped; and a general alarm being given, every person who had a horse rode into the woods, in the hopes of apprehending him; and Demba Sego begged the use of my horse for the same purpose. I readily consented; and in about an hour, they all returned with the slave, who was severely flogged, and afterwards put in irons."†

Here, again, is a specimen of the internal slave trade:

* Chap. XVIII. † Chap. VI.

"I was walking barefoot, driving my horse, when I was met by a coffle [gang or company] of slaves, about seventy in number, coming from Sego. They were tied together by their necks with thongs of a bullock's hide, twisted like a rope, seven slaves upon a thong, and a man with a musket between every seven. Many of the slaves were ill-conditioned, and a great number of them women. These slaves were going to Morocco, by the way of Ludamar and the Great Desert."*

And here it may be observed, that the sufferings endured by the slaves in crossing the Desert of Sahara are described as being even greater than those experienced in the "middle passage" across the Atlantic. "Driven by Arab merchants to the north of Africa, through the deep and burning sands of Sahara, scantily supplied with water, they sink in great numbers under their sufferings. Major Denham and his companions saw, in their journeyings, melancholy proofs of the horrors attending this 'middle passage' over land. They at one time halted near a well, around which were lying more than one hundred human skeletons, some of them with the skin still remaining on their bones. 'They were only *blacks*,' said the Arabs, when they observed the horror of the travelers; and they began to knock about the limbs and skulls with the butt-ends of their guns. Denham says they counted in another place one hundred and seven skeletons. In other instances they passed sixty or eighty skeletons a-day, scattered along over that dreary waste.—'While,' says Denham, 'I was dozing on

* Chap. XV.

my horse, about noon, overcome by the heat of the sun, I was suddenly awakened by a crashing under my feet; and found that my steed had stepped on the perfect skeletons of two human beings, cracking their brittle bones under his feet; and by one trip of his foot separating a skull from the trunk, it rolled on like a ball before him.' About the walls of El-Hamar, they saw many; and among the rest, the skeletons of two young females, faithful friends it would seem, even in death, for they lay with their fleshless arms still clasped round each other."* We hear much of the horrors of the slave-trade on the western coast, and of the "middle passage" across the Atlantic; but were that all put an end to to-morrow, the sufferings of the Africans would be but very partially relieved, while the internal slave-trade in their own country is still so actively going on. ' We must extend our plans and push our efforts far beyond American slavery, and even beyond the Atlantic slave-trade,—into the heart of Africa itself,— if we would strike at the root of the evil, and put an end to the sufferings of humanity that spring from this source. American slavery is but a drop in the bucket; it is merely one of the branches of African slavery.

Here is a description of the manner in which these wretched slaves, about to be driven across the Desert, are procured:

"In Bornou, where the slave-trade is carried on to an immense extent and is the principal traffic, the mode in which slaves are procured is very summary.

* Freeman's *Plea for Africa*, Conversation VI.

A caravan of Moorish merchants arrives and offers goods for slaves. If there are no slaves on hand, they must be procured. The Sultan immediately collects his forces, marches into the country of some harmless tribe, burns their villages, destroys their fields and flocks, massacres the infirm and old, and returns with as many able-bodied prisoners as he can seize. Sometimes 3,000 have been obtained in a single '*ghrazie,*' as these expeditions are called."* What a picture of savagery and cruelty is this! And the slave-trade across the Great Desert, sustained by these enormities, has been going on (according to Bancroft) since A.D. 990,—nearly nine hundred years.

Here may be introduced another extract from Mungo Park, which presents a view at once of the internal slave-trade of Africa, and of the sufferings which the slaves sometimes endure in their long journeys from the interior to the western coast. The person, Karfa, mentioned in the extract, was a slatee or African slave-dealer, by no means cruel, but on the whole a kind-hearted man, who showed great kindness to Park, and was the means, indeed, of his being enabled to reach the coast on his return, and thus take ship for home. The narrative simply exhibits the wretched customs of a country where a "prime slave" is the ordinary standard of value.

"On the 24th of January, Karfa returned to Kamalia with a number of people, and thirteen prime slaves whom he had purchased.—The slaves which Karfa had brought with him were all of

Freeman's *Plea for Africa*, Conversation VI.

them prisoners of war; they had been taken by the Bambarra army and carried to Sego, where some of them had remained three years in irons. From Sego they were sent in company with a number of captives up the Niger in two large canoes, and offered for sale at Yammina, Bambakoo, and Kancaba; at which places, the greater number of the captives were bartered for gold dust, and the remainder sent forward to Kankaree.

"Eleven of these [that is, of the thirteen] confessed to me that they had been slaves from their infancy, but the other two refused to give any account of their former condition. They were all very inquisitive, but they viewed me at first with looks of horror, and repeatedly asked if my countrymen were cannibals. They were very desirous to know what became of the slaves after they had crossed the salt-water. I told them that they were employed in cultivating the land; but they would not believe me, and one of them, putting his hand upon the ground, said, with great simplicity, 'Have you really got such ground as this to set your feet upon?' A deeply-rooted idea, that the whites purchase negroes for the purpose of devouring them, or of selling them to others, that they may be devoured hereafter, naturally makes the slaves contemplate a journey towards the coast with great terror, insomuch that the slatees are forced to keep them constantly in irons, and watch them very closely, to prevent their escape. They are commonly secured by putting the right leg of one and the left of another into the same pair of fetters. By supporting the fetters with a string, they can walk, though very slowly. Every four slaves are likewise fastened together by the necks with a strong rope of twisted thongs, and in the night an additional pair of fetters is put on their hands, and sometimes a light iron chain is put round their necks. Such of them as evince marks of discontent are secured in a different manner. A thick billet of wood is cut about three feet long, and a smooth notch being made on one side of it, the ankle of the slave is bolted to the smooth part by means of a strong iron staple, one prong of which passes on each side of the ankle.—In other respects the treatment of the slaves during their stay at Kamalia was far from being harsh or cruel. They were led out in their fetters every morning to the shade of the tamarind-tree, where they were encouraged to play at games of hazard, and sing diverting songs to keep up their spirits; for though some of them sustained the hardships of their situation with amazing fortitude, the greater part were very much dejected, and would sit all day in a sort of sullen melancholy, with their eyes fixed upon the ground.

"The long wished-for day of our departure at length arrived: and the slatees having taken the irons from their slaves, assembled with them at the door or Karfa's house, where the bundles were all tied up, and every one had his load assigned him. The coffle [company], on its departure from Kamalia, consisted of twenty-seven slaves for sale, the property of Karfa and four other slatees; but we were afterwards joined by five at Maraboo, and three at Bala, making in all thirty-five slaves. As many of the slaves had remained for years in irons, the sudden exertion of walking quick with heavy loads upon their heads occasioned spasmodic contractions of the legs; and we had not proceeded above a mile, before it was found necessary to take two of them from the rope, and allow them to walk more slowly until we reached Maraboo, a walled village, where some people were waiting to join the coffle.—From this place, we continued to travel with the greatest expedition, and in the afternoon crossed two small branches of the Kokoro. About sunset, we came in sight of a considerable town, nearly square, situated in the middle of a large and well cultivated plain: before we entered the town, we halted until the people who had fallen behind came up. During this day's travel, two slaves, *a woman and a girl*, belonging to a slatee at Bala, were so much fatigued that they could not keep up with the coffle. They were *severely whipped*, and dragged along until about three o'clock in the afternoon, when they were both affected with vomiting, by which it was discovered that they had eaten clay. This practice is by no means uncommon amongst the negroes,—but whether it arises from a vitiated appetite, or from a settled intention to destroy themselves, I cannot affirm.

"April 24th.—Before day-break, the bushreens [Mahometans] said their morning-prayers, and most of the free people drank a little *moening* (a sort of gruel), part of which was likewise given to such of the slaves as appeared least able to sustain the fatigues of the day. One of Karfa's female slaves was very sulky, and when some gruel was offered to her, she refused to drink it. As soon as day dawned, we set out, and traveled the whole morning over a wild and rocky country, by which my feet were much bruised, and I was sadly apprehensive that I should not be able to keep up with the coffle during the day; but I was in great measure relieved from this anxiety, when I observed that others were more exhausted than myself. In particular the woman-slave who had refused victuals in the morning, began now to lag behind, and complain dreadfully of pains in her legs. Her load was taken from her, and given to another slave, and she was ordered to keep in the front of the coffle. About eleven o'clock, as we were resting by a small rivulet, some of the people discovered a hive of bees in a hollow tree, and they were proceeding to obtain the honey, when the largest swarm I ever beheld flew out, and attacking the people of the coffle, made us fly in all directions. I took the alarm first, and I believe was the only person who escaped with impunity. When our enemies thought fit to desist from pursuing us, and every person was employed in picking out the stings he had received, it was discovered that the poor woman above mentioned, whose name was Nealee, was not come up; and as many of the slaves in their retreat had left their bundles behind them, it became necessary for some persons to return and bring them. In order to do this with safety, fire was set to the grass a considerable way to the eastward of the hive; and the wind driving the fire furiously along, the party pushed through the smoke, and recovered the bundles. They likewise brought with them poor Nealee, whom they found lying by the rivulet. She was very much exhausted, and had crept to the stream in hopes to defend herself from the bees, by throwing water over her body; but this proved ineffectual, for she was stung in the most dreadful manner.

"When the slatees had picked out the stings as well as they could, she was washed with water, and then rubbed with bruised leaves; but the wretched woman obstinately refused to proceed any further, declaring that she would rather die than walk another step. As entreaties and threats were used in vain, the *whip* was at length applied; and after bearing patiently a few strokes, she started up, and walked with tolerable expedition for four or five hours longer, when she made an attempt to run away from the coffle, but was so very weak that she fell down in the grass. Though she was unable to rise, the whip was a second time applied, but without effect, upon which Karfa desired two of the slatees to place her upon the ass which carried our dried provisions; but she could not sit erect, and, the ass being very refractory, it was found impossible to carry her forward in that manner. The slatees, however, were unwilling to abandon her, the day's journey being nearly ended; they therefore made a sort of litter of bamboo canes, upon which she was placed, and tied on it with slips of bark; the litter was carried upon the heads of two slaves, one walking before the other, and they were followed by two others, who relieved them occasionally. In this manner the woman was carried forward until it was dark, when we reached a stream of water, at the foot of a high hill, and here we stopped for the night, and set about preparing our supper. As we had eaten only one handful of meal since the preceding night, and had traveled all day in a hot sun, many of the slaves who had loads upon their heads, were very much fatigued, and some of them *snapped their fingers*, which among the negroes is a sure sign of desperation. The slatees immediately put them all in irons; and such of them as had evinced signs of great despondency were kept apart from the rest, and had their hands tied. In the morning they were found greatly recovered.

"April 25th.—At day-break, poor Nealee was awakened, but her limbs were now become so stiff and painful that she could neither walk nor stand. She was therefore lifted, like a corpse, upon the back of the ass, and the slatees endeavoured to secure her in that situation by fastening her hands together under the ass's neck, and her feet under the belly, with long slips of bark; but the ass was so very unruly that no sort of treatment could induce him to proceed with his load, and as Nealee used no sort of exertion to prevent herself from falling, she was quickly thrown off, and had one of her legs much bruised. Every attempt to carry her forward being thus found ineffectual, the general cry of the coffle was *Kang-tegi, kang-tegi!* ("cut her throat, cut her throat!") an operation I did not wish to see performed, and therefore marched onwards with the foremost of the coffle. I had not walked above a mile, when one of Karfa's domestic slaves came up to me, with poor Nealee's garment on the end of his bow, and exclaimed *Nealee affeeleeta* ("Nealee is lost!") I asked him whether the slatees had given him the garment, as a reward for cutting her throat; he replied, that Karfa would not consent to that measure, but had left her on the road, where undoubtedly she soon perished, and was probably devoured by wild beasts."*

What a picture is this! It is scarcely surpassed by the sad tale of "Old Prue"† or even that of poor "Uncle Tom" himself. Yet such distressing circumstances are doubtless occurring throughout Africa daily and continually, and have been for a thousand years past. It is not merely, as before shown, in connection with the Atlantic slave-trade, carried on by the whites, that such things take place, but also in the Great Desert slave-trade carried on by the Moors; and independently of both of these—they occur among the negroes themselves in the heart of the continent. It is, in fact, the Africans themselves who are the cause of their own sufferings. It is a great error to suppose that this distressing state of things originated with the whites, however much it may have been aggravated by them. Had there been no internal slavery and slave-trade, there could have been no external. Had the Africans not been long addicted, previously, to buying and selling each other, within their own continent, they would never have been found willing, or could have been made willing, to sell their fellows, as they do, to the white traders upon the coast. Here is the true secret and explanation of the cause of Africa's suffering from the slave-trade and slavery,—namely, *Africa's own state of moral degradation.*‡

* Park's *Travels in the Interior of Africa*, chap. xxv.
† See *Uncle Tom's Cabin*, chaps. xviii. xix.
‡ To show how distinctly the Africans themselves are the cause of their own enslavement, and of the existence and continuance of the slave-trade, may be mentioned the striking fact, that in 1796, when, in consequence of the French Revolution and the subsequent European

In the following passage, which will conclude, for the present, our extracts from Park, there is a brief summary of the facts already stated in reference to the number and general condition of the slaves. He is speaking here particularly of the Mandingoes; but as shown from previous extracts, the same statements apply to Africa in general. The writer, after a description of the manners of the inhabitants, remarks:

"In the account which I have thus given of the natives, the reader must bear in mind, that my observations apply chiefly to persons of free condition, who constitute, I suppose, not more than one-fourth part of the inhabitants at large; the other *three-fourths* are in a state of hopeless and hereditary slavery; and are employed in cultivating the land, in the care of cattle, and in servile offices of all kinds, much in the same manner as the slaves in the West Indies. I was told, however, that the Mandingo master can neither deprive his slave of life, nor sell him to a stranger, without

wars, the trade had greatly declined, the negro King of Dahomey sent a special embassy, consisting of his brother and son, to Portugal, for the purpose of reviving the traffic, and of concluding a treaty with Portugal to that end. In truth, the touching pictures which have been drawn by some of the English poets, of the white man landing at night, and kidnapping the poor African,—if not entire fictions, yet, at most, describe cases that must be mere exceptions. It is well known that without the active coöperation of the negroes themselves, the white trader could not procure a single cargo of slaves; and had not slavery and the slave-trade existed most extensively in Africa before, such an attempt on the part of the whites would probably never have been made or thought of. It should at the same time be remembered, that these facts afford no justification whatever to the unprincipled trader, who takes advantage of this low moral condition of the natives, to carry on the abominable traffic in human beings: they are adduced simply to show the true cause of the existence of this lamentable state of things.

first calling a *palaver* on his conduct, or in other words, bringing him to a public trial. But this degree of protection is extended only to the native or domestic slave. Captives taken in war, and those unfortunate victims who are condemned to slavery for crimes or insolvency,—and in short, all those unhappy people who are brought down from the interior countries for sale —have no security whatever, but may be treated and disposed of in all respects as the owner thinks proper."*

Such is a view of the internal state and condition of Africa—as it is, and as, according to all accounts, it has been for ages, and from the earliest times. According to the representation of the traveler above quoted, (and no one, perhaps, has had a better opportunity both for inquiry and observation), nearly or quite three-fourths of the inhabitants of Africa—so far as any exploration has been made—are held in a state of bondage, of absolute slavery and subjection to the remaining fourth. The population of Africa has been roughly estimated at from 120 to 160 millions: taking the mean between these two—140 millions—we have, for three-fourths of this number, 105 millions; showing, thus, the existence of upwards of *one hundred millions of slaves* within the borders of that benighted continent. What an enormous number is this! How insignificant, in comparison, seem the numbers in the New World —the three millions in North America, and the two millions in Brazil!†

* Chap. II.

† Dr. Livingston's *African Travels*, which have appeared since the above was written, show a somewhat better state of things in Southern Africa; but it appears, nevertheless, from that work, that slavery very generally exists, and that "a *man*" is a common article of barter.

From the above extracts, too, we learn what is the condition of that vast multitude; that, while the "domestic slaves," or those born in the master's house, have some privileges, all the rest, the captives taken in war, all that are purchased, all who become slaves through crime or even through insolvency, are absolutely at the disposal of their masters, to be treated with any degree of severity to which the caprice of their masters may subject them. And under masters in such a state of barbarism, we may believe that they must often cruelly suffer,—as, indeed, the writer expressly states to be the case. He describes to us the condition of the slaves among the Moorish tribes— the females the sport of the ill temper of their mistresses—pounding the corn and dressing the victuals under the combined heats of the burning sun, the sand, and the fire; treated with less indulgence even than the beasts of burthen,—compelled to bring water a long distance for the supply of the very horses, rather than "give the latter the trouble" of going to the wells to drink: "with all this," the writer remarks, "they are badly fed, and oftentimes cruelly treated: the condition of these poor captives is deplorably wretched." We have seen with what barbarous disregard they are treated when dead; the body of the poor slave-boy dragged by a leg and arm, and thrown into a pit. Those who could treat with such insulting unconcern the remains of their dead slaves, we may be sure could not have been very tender to them while living. We have, too, an account of the pursuit of a fugitive slave, hunted in the usual manner, with man and horse

—and the severe flogging he was subjected to, for the attempt to recover his liberty. We have, also, pictures of the internal slave-trade in Africa—its universal prevalence, and the distresses and sufferings with which it is accompanied. We behold the poor slaves, many of them women, yoked together by the neck, setting out on their terrible journey across the Great Desert,—the skeletons of hundreds who have preceded them lying in their path. We see, too, the awful ravages and desolations inflicted by the King of Bornou and other negro chiefs, to procure these slaves, setting peaceful villages on fire, putting to death the old and infirm, and carrying off the young into hopeless slavery. Again, we see others, taken prisoners in war, lying for years in chains in prison, and then taken out to be sent up the Niger, to be sold as slaves at the various towns along its banks; and the remainder, not thus sold, sent off on a painful march to the distant Western Coast. In a word, we find here a complete state of slavery, with all its usual concomitants, "regular slave-markets," negro slave-merchants (slatees), bad treatment, semi-starvation, suffering in all forms. And withal, we have the painful thought that all this suffering is continually inflicted on such a vast number of human beings—probably upwards of *one hundred millions*—and that this course of things has been going on now for ages!

And where, now, is the remedy? In the ordinary course of things, none—none probable—none seemingly possible. Slavery under Europeans, or their descendants in the New World, slavery in Christian lands, must necessarily be a temporary thing: its abolition is a mere question of time. The light of Christian truth, shining steadily upon the mind, is ever gently yet powerfully exercising its influence on a people's heart, and appealing to their conscience, till at length entering, and bringing with it the fire of love, it will melt the human soul to pity, and dissolve all cruel bonds. So it has been doing in ages past, and so it will continue to do, till every yoke is broken, and all the oppressed go free. So it has been in Europe, and so it will yet be in America. But where the light of Christian truth is not spread abroad—where the law of Christian love is not known, but man is left to his natural darkness and selfishness—what hope, what prospect is there, for the slave? None—none. The chains will still clank on, and the iron of oppression enter into the soul, through summer and winter, through revolving years and rolling ages still. This is the condition of the continent of Africa. For ages and ages past have those enslaved millions been suffering, and crying to their *fetiches* and idol-gods in vain. Their chains could not be broken; for nothing but the lightning power of truth could do it, and that truth had not reached them. He alone who came to "bring out the prisoners from the prison, and them that sit in darkness out of the prison-house" —He alone could do it: but alas! He had not come to them, He was not known to them. The Divine Savior had, indeed, come into the world,—yet He or His coming had not been heard of by the benighted millions of Africa. No light of Gospel truth had penetrated to them. They seemed, indeed, to be quite out of the line of its course: it was crossing the world, like the sun, on a belt from east to west; but poor Africa was far to the southward, out of its way, and seemingly beyond the reach of its influence. Or, if its missionaries sought, in their benevolence, to get to them, they were stopped by the Great Desert on the North, by the deadly malaria on the West: the white man could not live in that atmosphere and under that tropical sun.

Was there no hope, then, for that dark continent? Must "Ethiopia ever stretch out her hands" in vain? Had God "forgotten to be gracious?"—had the good Savior of mankind forsaken so large a portion of His creatures? No! He had not forgotten or forsaken them. In His own time and in His own manner He was preparing deliverance for them. The means, too, were seemingly hard and strange—such as could not have been thought of, such as could hardly be believed, by man. Such is ever the manner of the Divine working: "His ways are not as our ways, nor his thoughts as our thoughts." It is impossible that they should be; for He knows all, while man knows but an infinitesimal part: He beholds the universe at a glance, while man sees but the single thing just before his eyes. It is not till effects begin to show themselves, that man has an understanding of causes: it is not till results begin to appear, that man begins to have a dawning perception of God's great designs.

As Moses, of old, was in God's providence permitted to be taken away by the daughter of Pharaoh, that he might afterwards return to his people, replenished with "all the wisdom of the Egyptians;"—as the children of Israel were suffered to be held long in bondage, far from the country of their fathers and the promised land,—that they might afterwards return thither, prepared to become instruments for restoring the true worship of Jehovah:—so have the thousands and tens of thousands of Africans been permitted, we may believe, to be taken away from their native land to the New World,—to the end that, in an after-time, they or their descendants might return, civilized and Christianized, prepared to become the favored instruments for introducing into that benighted continent the lights of civilization and of the Gospel,—breaking up at once the reign of idolatry and of slavery, and spreading far and wide the knowledge of the true God, and, with it, the true spirit of freedom. It was the only way in which that great end could be accomplished: and we can now see that it was the plan of profound and infinite Wisdom.

SECTION IV.

THE REPUBLIC OF LIBERIA.

THE great work of African restitution has already begun. Silently and unobtrusively,—like all the great doings of the Divine One—and almost unobserved by many and by most, has the work been steadily going on, now for nearly forty years. It had, like all great things, a small beginning. A single benevolent individual, the Rev. Robert Finley, of New Jersey, United States, was the first who conceived (or at least, the first actively to carry into execution) a plan for restoring the negroes in America to the land of their fathers. "For years," says an interesting writer, "this eminent Christian had viewed the condition of the free colored population in the United States with sympathizing interest, and the whole vigor of his intellect was aroused to form plans for their relief. Among the exiled children of Africa, this good man saw not merely the heirs to a temporal but to an eternal existence; not those possessing merely the virtues of natural and social affection, but also capacities for the high improvements and joys of an immortal state. Early in the year 1815, he expressed himself to a friend as follows: 'The longer I live to see the wretchedness of men, the more I admire the virtue of those who devise, and patiently labor to execute, plans for the relief of the wretched. Under th w, the state of the *free blacks* has very much occ ꭎied my mind. Their number is increasing greatly, and, as it appears to me, their wretchedness also. Everything connected with their condition, including their color, is against them; nor is there much prospect that their state can ever be greatly ameliorated while they continue among us. Could not the rich and benevolent devise means to form a colony on some part of the coast of Africa, similar to the one at Sierra Leone, which might gradually induce many free blacks to go and settle, devising for them the means of getting there, and of protection and support till they are established? Could they be sent back to Africa, a threefold benefit would arise. We should be cleared of them; we should send to Africa a population partly civilized and Christianized, for its benefit; and our blacks themselves would be in a much better situation.' Mr. Finley was satisfied of the practicability and utility of the project; and encouraged by the opinions of others, resolved to make a great effort to carry his benevolent views into effect. In making preparatory arrangements, he spent a considerable part of the fall of 1816; and, determining to test the popularity and in some measure the practicability of the whole system, he at length introduced the subject to public notice in the city of Washington. For this purpose he visited several members of Congress, the President, the Heads of Departments, and others. His conversation and zeal are said to have done much in drawing attention to the subject, and in conciliating many who at first appeared opposed. He proposed a special season of prayer in reference to the object, and several pious persons met him for the purpose of spending an hour in such an exercise. When told that some were incredulous, and that some ridiculed the plan proposed, he replied, '*I know this scheme is from God.*'"*

It *was* from God. Begun thus in a spirit of humble dependence on the Divine blessing, it was upheld by the Divine support, and succeeded. In furtherance of the great object, a society was formed at Washington, in December, 1816, under the name of the "American Colonization Society." It was composed of some of the best and wisest men of the nation, north and south. Soon, also, the cause attracted attention in England; and some of the truest friends of Africa and of the slave interested themselves in it, foreseeing in these small beginnings a great future. The venerable Clarkson, speaking of it some years afterwards, thus wrote: "For myself, I am free to say, that of all things that have been going on in our favor since 1787, when the abolition of the slave-trade was first seriously proposed, that which is going on in the United States is the most important. It surpasses everything that has yet occurred. No sooner had your colony been established on Cape Montserado than there appeared a

* *Plea for Africa; or, Familiar Conversations on the Subject of Slavery and Colonization*, by the Rev. J. Freeman, Philadelphia. We would warmly recommend this book to general perusal: it contains much interesting information on the subjects of slavery, the slave-trade, and the colonization of Africa; and it is written in the best spirit.

disposition among the owners of slaves to give them freedom voluntarily and without compensation, and allow them to be sent to the land of their fathers; so that you have *many thousands redeemed, without any cost of their redemption.* To me this is truly astonishing. Can this have taken place without the intervention of the Spirit of God?" A distinguished British nobleman, Lord Althorp, publicly pronounced the foundation of the Colony of Liberia "one of the greatest events of modern times." A society in aid of the cause was formed in England, headed by persons of the first distinction, denominated the "British African Colonization Society." The framers of this Association, it was declared, "consider the plan of the American Colonization Society as admirably adapted to introduce Christianity and civilization among the natives of Africa, and to extirpate the slave-trade, which the moral efforts of Great Britain and other powers have been unable to suppress."*

The cause, it is true, met with opposition in some quarters,—as what good cause ever did not? The violent defenders of slavery were opposed to it, because it tended towards the emancipation of the slaves; while, on the other hand, the over-zealous opponents of slavery attacked it, on the ground that its tendency was to check emancipation—an astonishing assertion, in view of the fact stated above by Clarkson, namely, that the effect of it had already been to cause numbers of slaves to be voluntarily emancipated. This opposi-

* Freeman's *Plea for Africa*, Conversation XX. At a later period, Clarkson and many other English friends of African colonization, cooled in their zeal for the cause; but it was through the misrepresentations of its enemies.

tion of extremities on both sides proved the cause to be one of those truly wise and móderate ones, which, respecting all interests, and just to all, move on calmly but firmly, under the God who leads them, to ultimate triumph and glory. This very opposition, moreover, will have been of the greatest service to the final success of the cause, and a signal proof of the watchful care of Divine Providence. Had there been, at the commencement of operations, one general voice of praise, approbation, and encouragement, on all sides— from whites and from blacks, together—the cause would probably have been ruined. Such a mass of emigrants, such a flood of the colored population, would have been poured on the infant colony, as would have overwhelmed it. The whole history of colonization shows that this would have been the result. The French attempted to colonize Cayenne with a grand body of 12,000 men—and a great part of them miserably perished of starvation. But the pilgrims of New England, few in number, landing in the depth of winter on an inhospitable shore—yet managed to maintain themselves, and prepared the way for others to follow, till a great nation sprang into existence. So the African colony, beginning with a few emigrants, and these preparing the way for more, had time to take firm root in the soil,—and growing little by little, has now, after nearly forty years, become so strong and flourishing, as to be able to receive an immigration of large numbers without injury.

The first effective settlement was made in the year 1822, at Cape Montserado or Mesurado, a lofty promontory on the African coast, about 250 miles south of Sierra Leone. The colony was aptly named LIBERIA, the land of the *freed*. The chief settlement received the name of MONROVIA, after President Monroe, then at the head of the United States Government. The soil and climate are described as most rich and delightful, and the scenery, in many parts, beautiful and picturesque even to grandeur. "A more fertile soil," says Mr. Freeman, "or a more productive country, I suspect it would be difficult to find on the face of the earth. Its hills and plains are covered with a verdure that never fades; the productions of nature keep on in their growth through all seasons of the year; and even the natives of the country, almost without farming tools or skill, with very little labor, raise more grain and vegetables than they can consume, and often more than they can sell. Mr. Park, the traveler, says 'A'l the rich and valuable productions both of the East and West Indies might easily be naturalized, and brought to the utmost perfection in the tropical parts of this immense continent.—It was not possible for me to behold the wonderful fertility of the soil, the vast herds of cattle proper both for labor and for food, and a variety of other circumstances favorable to colonization and agriculture,—and reflect, withal, on the means which presented themselves of a vast inland navigation,—without lamenting that a country so gifted and favored by nature should remain in its present savage and neglected state.'

"The colonists," continues the writer above named, "have all the domestic animals which are found in this country. They raise a great variety of vegetables and tropical fruits. Coffee grows spontaneously and of an excellent kind. The attention of some of the most respectable colonists has been turned to its cultivation, and twenty thousand coffee-trees have been planted by a single individual. The indigo plant is indigenous, and grows wild almost everywhere on the coast. Cotton is easily cultivated, and the crops are productive. The sugar-cane is found on many parts of the coast, and may be cultivated in Liberia. Rice is easy of cultivation, and has long been the principal article of food to the natives. Bananas, of an excellent and delicious kind, plantains, oranges fine-flavoured and very large, and limes, are common; maize or Indian-corn ripens in three months, and succeeds well; pine-apples are very good and in great abundance; cocoanut-trees flourish there; pumpkins, squashes, cucumbers, water-melons, and musk-melons, arrive at great perfection in that climate. Cassada and yams are found in all parts of the coast, and are much used for food; palm-oil is produced in abundance; also tamarinds of various kinds; gum-senegal and copal are articles of export in great quantities; pepper, and a variety of other spices, as cayenne, ginger, nutmegs, and cinnamon, are common on the coast; several valuable dye-woods are found, of which camwood and barwood are exported in considerable quantities; *gold* abounds in many parts of Africa, and the amount exported may be greatly increased; ivory is also a great article of commerce, and timber of almost every quality. All these and many other productions are found in Africa, and are or may become sources of advantage and profit to the Liberian colony."*

* *Plea for Africa*, Conversation XXI.

With such resources, the commerce of Liberia is already very considerable: indeed, it seems to have become such at a very early period,—thus presenting great prospects for the future. As long ago as 1826— in six months, from January to June, of that year— "the nett profits on wood and ivory alone, passing through the hands of the settlers, were upwards of thirty thousand dollars (£6,000). In 1829, we find the exports of African produce amounting to sixty thousand dollars. In 1831, forty-six vessels, twenty-one of which were American, visited the colony. During the year ending May 1, 1832, fifty-nine vessels had visited the port of Monrovia, and the exports during the same period amounted to one hundred and twenty-five thousand dollars, and the imports to eighty thousand dollars. A portion of the colonists are continually and actively engaged in trade with the natives, disposing of English, American, and other goods, and receiving in return dye-woods, ivory, hides, palm-oil, tortoise-shell, rice, and gold, which become articles of exportation, affording great profit. Even now the harbor of Monrovia presents, at times, a most animating scene of commercial activity and enterprise. One may often see there the harbor whitened with sails—vessels anchoring or taking their departure, loading and unloading; you behold warehouses stored with rich cargoes; you hear the busy hum of industry; you observe the alert movements of active men, once most of them sluggish slaves! Freedom has transformed them."*

The climate of Liberia is tropical, and therefore

* Ibid.

well adapted to the condition of the colored race, who seem indeed intended by nature for such a climate and for no other. Where the white man sickens and dies from the heat, there the negro sports and rejoices, and is the most strong and vigorous. "The city of Monrovia," says Mr. Freeman, "is seventy feet above the sea; and the temperature is mild and agreeable, the thermometer not varying more than from 68 to 87 degrees, and the inhabitants enjoying most of the time a refreshing sea-breeze." Of another settlement, formed at Cape Palmas, called New Maryland, it is stated that "the situation is high, open, free from any surrounding marshes, and most favorable to health." "As to the climate," says Mr. Buchanan, Agent of the 'Young Men's Colonization Society of Pennsylvania,' and late Governor of the Colony at Bassa Cove, "it is entirely a mistake to suppose that it is destructive of health." He went there "with his mind filled with the graphic pictures, drawn by the prolific pencil of the poet, of burning sands, mephitic marshes, and scorching winds, but saw neither." He was "struck with the beautiful luxuriance of the soil; and as to the heat, the result of the regular thermometrical observations taken at Bassa Cove was, that in the hot season the mercury ranged between 80 and 88 degrees Fahrenheit, and in the cold or wet season it seldom falls below 70 degrees. There is besides a continual and refreshing breeze from the sea during the day, and from the land during the night." During his residence at Bassa Cove, not a single death had occurred in the colony.* Again he

* *Plea for Africa*, Conversation XXIV.

says, in a letter to the Corresponding Secretary of the above-named Society, "You may congratulate yourself on your steadfast affection for Bassa Cove, for indeed it is a paradise. The climate is abundantly good, the soil prolific and various in its productions, the rivers abound in excellent fish and very superior oysters, and the water is pure and wholesome. Our position is somewhat remarkable, having a river in our rear, the ocean in front, and the magnificent St. John's sweeping past on our right. The luxuriant and various foliage which overhangs the banks of the river, and recedes back into the interminable forests, gives a perpetual freshness to the scene, which ever animates the beholder. In America it is difficult to conceive of African scenery without picturing to our imagination a plentiful supply of burning sand, with here and there a fiery serpent; but what a pleasing reversion the feelings undergo, when for the first time we witness the reality; then the imaginary arid scene, with its odious accompaniments, is exchanged for the broad river of blue waters, the stately forest, and the ever verdant landscape, and all Nature charms with her ever varying, yet ever beautiful and living riches."*

A still grander view of Liberian scenery is presented us in the following extract from the report of Mr. Whitehurst, a commissioner sent by the Colonial Government on a visit into the interior. It is descriptive of a port of the country, about eighty or a hundred miles back from Monrovia. Mr. Whitehurst remarks, —"Everything conspires to render this spot desirable for human happiness, if the propensity for war which

* *Plea*, Conversation XXV.

the people [the natives] have could be got over.—Groups of cheerful beings were passed through, either planting or grubbing; while at the towns the women were generally employed in spinning cotton. Cotton grows abundantly throughout the country, and every town is furnished more or less with the apparatus for dyeing and weaving. The sugar-cane, too, we observed frequently, while the plantain and banana were in the greatest profusion. The first notice, at times, that we could have of our proximity to a town, would be the dense and beautiful foliage of those trees, giving us notice of human habitations. We approached Talma through beautiful walks of lofty and magnificent trees, very thickly interspersed with those of camwood, whose fragrant blossoms imparted delightful aroma to the atmosphere. The situation of Bo Poro," he continues, "is very obscure, being located in a valley formed by a chain of double mountains, completely encircling it, and giving to their elevation a remarkable similitude to the seats of a theatre. The scenery by which the town is surrounded is magnificently grand; and as far as the eye can see, you discern mountain above mountain, until they are lost in the distance. The chain runs regularly for some miles; then a portion more lofty than the rest towers aloft; whilst from base to summit the eye can behold but one expanse of the greenest foliage. Upon the whole, the scenery is more magnificent than any that I remember having seen."

Let us turn now from this brief survey of the soil, climate, and scenery of Liberia, to an examination of the interior and domestic condition of the colony.

As long ago as 1831, Elliot Cresson, Esq., the generous and fast friend of the African race,—in an address delivered at the fourteenth anniversary of the Colonization Society, thus spoke of its general condition and prospects:—"Only nine years have elapsed since the little band of colonists landed at the cape [Mesurado], and a nation has already sprung into existence;—a nation destined to secure to Ethiopia the fulfilment of the glorious prophecy made in her behalf. Already have kings thrown down their crowns at the feet of the infant republic; and formed with her a holy alliance, for the purpose of exchanging the guilty traffic in human flesh and blood for legitimate commerce, equal laws, civilization and religion.

> 'From many an ancient river,
> From many a palmy plain,
> They call us to deliver
> Their land from errors chain.'

They ask for schools, factories, churches. Nearly 2,000 freemen have kindled a beacon-fire at Monrovia, to cast a broad blaze of light into the dark recesses of that benighted land. The annals of colonization may be triumphantly challenged for a parallel. Five years of preliminary operations for surveying the coast, propitiating the natives, and selecting the most eligible site; numerous agents subsequently employed, ships chartered, the forest cleared; school-houses, factories, hospitals, churches, goverment buildings, and dwellings erected, and the many expenses requisite at home defrayed;—and yet, for every fifty dollars (£10) expended by our Society from its commencement, we have not only a settler to show, but an ample and fertile territory in reserve, where our future emigrants may sit under their own vines and fig-trees, with none to make them afraid. During the last year an amount nearly equal to the united expenditures in effecting these objects, has been exported by the colonists; and from Philadelphia alone *eleven* vessels have sailed, bearing to the land of their forefathers a large number of *slaves manumitted by the benevolence of their owners.*"—Truly may it be said, that the annals of colonization have no parallel to this. The Divine blessing appears plainly to have been with the cause.

"The chief town, MONROVIA," says Mr. Freeman (writing in 1837), "contains about five hundred houses and stores [dwellings and warehouses], a court-house, five churches—one Presbyterian, two Methodist, and two Baptist—three flourishing schools, one of which has upwards of a hundred scholars,—a temperance society, numbering upwards of five hundred members,—and about 1,500 inhabitants. The houses are generally well built, and of a pleasant appearance. The city is seventy feet above the sea, and the temperature mild and agreeable. The streets are one hundred feet wide, crossing each other at right angles. The harbor, which is formed by the mouth of the river, is convenient and spacious for vessels of moderate dimensions.

"Seven miles north of the outlet of the Mesurado is the river St. Paul's, on which is the town of CALDWELL. This town, after the plan of some American villages, has but one street, which is a mile and a half long, and is planted on each side with a beautiful row of plantain and banana trees. Caldwell is an agricultural establishment, and is flourishing. It has three churches, three day-schools, and three Sunday-schools. It is an interesting fact, that one of the native kings recently applied at one of these day-schools for the admission of twelve children; which request, however, could not be granted, as the school was already full.

"Between Caldwell and Monrovia, on Stockton Creek, is a settlement of recaptured Africans, called NEW GEORGIA. It was planted in part by the aid of the United States Government. It contains five hundred inhabitants, who, though they were once the miserable tenants, in chains, of the loathsome slave-ship, are now living in the enjoyment of the blessings of civilized and Christian life. This place has a church and near two hundred houses. Mr. Buchanan, agent of the 'Young Men's Society of Pennsylvania,' who visited this place, says respecting this settlement, 'The air of perfect neatness, thrift, and comfort, which everywhere prevails, affords a lovely commentary on the advancement which these interesting people have made in civilization and Christian order, under the patronage of the Colonization Society. Imagine to yourself some two or three hundred houses, with streets intersecting each other at regular distances, preserved clean as the best side-walk in Philadelphia, and lined with well planted hedges of cassava and plum; a school-house full of orderly children, neatly dressed and studiously engaged;—and then say whether I was guilty of extravagance in exclaiming as I did, after surveying this charming scene, that had the Colonization Society accomplished no more than has been done in the rescue from slavery and savage habits, of these happy people, I should have been well satisfied.'

"Twenty miles north-east of Monrovia, on the same river, at the foot of the highlands, is another flourishing town, called MILLSBURGH, containing about five hundred inhabitants, two churches, and one school, and rapidly increasing by new colonists. Millsburgh has peculiar advantages, enabling it to become the commercial medium between the interior and the seacoast. The land is fertile, and the forests abound with excellent timber. The town is represented as very neat and healthy. Another town of recent settlement is MARSHALL.

"Another considerable settlement in Liberia is the very flourishing colony formed under the patronage of the Maryland Colonization Society, and also fostered by the State—at Cape Palmas—called NEW MARYLAND. This colony is advantageously located, and promises to excel in agriculture. Its situation is high, open, free from any surrounding marshes, and most favorable to health. Its inhabitants are described as temperate, intelligent, and industrious; and as giving evidence of mental as well as physical energy, that greatly encourages the confident hope and expectation that they will yet occupy an honourable rank in the civilized world.

"Besides these, there are the flourishing settlements more recently commenced at Edina and Bassa Cove, the one beautifully situated on the south, and the other on the north, side of the St. John's, near its mouth. Also, about eighty miles south-east from Bassa Cove, on the river Sinon, the MISSISSIPPI Colonization Society have purchased a territory and commenced a colony. The LOUISIANA Society propose the settlement of a colony on the opposite side of the same river. VIRGINIA, too, by her State Colonization Society has resolved to plant a colony upon the African coast, within the Liberian territory, to bear the name of *New Virginia*. KENTUCKY also has a prosperous colony there. And, indeed, many of the States have in Liberia distinct colonies, lining the coast of Western Africa, for many hundred miles,—thus furnishing a barrier to the approach of the slaver on the one side, whilst on the other they pour the light of civilization and Christianity upon benighted millions."*

Dr. Rainey, surgeon of the U. S. steam-frigate Niagara, which in 1858 was sent to Liberia to convey the slaves taken in the brig Echo, thus describes the country:—" No one can enter any part of the Republic of Liberia without being forcibly impressed with the mighty changes which this little voluntary society has made in that benighted land, and without blessing its founders and supporters, for having effectually redeemed six hundred miles of coast from the curse of the slave-trade.—Monrovia is a city of 3,000 inhabitants, a population as virtuous, orderly, and well conducted, as can be found in any country. The city is not healthily located, and hence bears but little of that impress of prosperity which is everywhere discernible throughout other portions of the Republic. I made a short visit up the St. Paul's river. The first few miles the banks are low and unhealthy, with malaria producing fever, though not worse than in

* *Plea for Africa*, Conversation XXI.

many places on the Missouri in America. But beyond seven miles the country becames high and rolling, on both banks, affording good water and healthful drainage. The river is most densely populated. The whole district is high and healthy. Fine brick houses appear all along the stream. The settlers seem to be thrifty and happy. I have nowhere else seen a place on earth so well fitted for the hopeful development of the colored man, as Liberia. A general remark to me by the colonists was, 'This, Sir, is a great country for darkies.'"*

We must here introduce an extract from a stirring address made by the colonists of Cape Palmas to their colored brethren in the United States. "We wish," say they, "to be candid. It is not every man that we can honestly advise or desire to come to this country. To those who are contented to live and educate their children as house-servants and lacqueys, we would say, stay where you are: here we have no masters to employ you. To the indolent, heedless, and slothful, we would say, tarry among the flesh-pots of Egypt: here we get our bread by the sweat of our brow. To drunkards and rioters we would say, come not to us: you never can become naturalized in a land where there are no grog-shops, and where temperance and order is the motto. To the timorous and suspicious we would say, stay where you have protectors: here we protect ourselves. But to the industrious, enterprising, and patriotic, of whatever occupation or enterprise—the mechanic, the merchant, the farmer, and especially the latter, we would counsel, advise, and

* *New York Herald,* of Dec. 11, 1858.

entreat to come over, and be one with us, and assist us in this glorious enterprise,—and enjoy with us that liberty to which we ever were, and to which the man of color ever must be, a stranger, in America. To the ministers of the Gospel, both white and colored, we would say, come over to this great harvest, and diffuse amongst us and our benighted neighbors the light of the Gospel, without which liberty is but slavery, and freedom perpetual bondage."*

In this connection, too, we may present an extract from a speech made in New York by a citizen of Liberia. At a meeting of the colored people held in that city, in June, 1850, Mr. Moore, of Liberia, made the following remarks :—

"Liberia offers, as its greatest gift, a free country. Our own race there are in power and in honor. You have heard of it, we know, and therefore prize it. We are a free and independent State, having a Constitution and Bill of Rights, like that of the United States. We do our own voting, while you, in most of this country, do not. I visited Washington city before I came here, and the condition of the poor people there pained my very heart. I wanted almost to force them to enjoy our privileges. I feel no inclination to return to Washington ; but if I do, it will be to induce or almost to compel some to go with me, for we will do them good. We are yet a small people and small population. Much has been done for us, and yet much remains to be done. We are, as it were, on the fringes of Africa. We are free, and rejoice at the present, and hope for the future. Our Republic may

* *Plea*, Conversation XXI.

yet extend, as do the United States, from one ocean to the other—from the Atlantic to the Indian. When we recall to mind the short time it has taken America to attain her greatness, what shall forbid to hope for such a future for ourselves, and that a vast emigration will yet take place to Liberia? What may not Liberia become? We expect much; we look and labor for much. Already Liberia, like a young Hercules, has strangled the hydra slave-trade for 300 or 400 miles along the coast, and is destined to complete the work. England is coöperating, and by keeping a blockade of Gallinas with two vessels, will aid in our present negotiations for that slave-mart; and when obtained, there will be none from the Senegal to the Niger, over 1,500 miles. We are proud of our country and its influences, because we enjoy there all the rights of man."*

In confirmation of the remarks of the speaker just quoted, in reference to the condition of freedom, equality, and consequent self-respect possessed by the citizens of Liberia — many of them once degraded slaves—we proceed to present a sketch of the political and civil condition of the colony (though the term *colony* is no longer suitable, as it has now become an independent State). The Colonization Society acted with great wisdom in their management of this important matter. In the year 1824, a form of government was submitted to the assembled colonists, and by them unanimously adopted. By this constitution, it was provided that the agent of the Society should be the

---

* New York *Journal of Commerce*. It may be added that the Gallinas territory has since been purchased and the slave-trade there entirely broken up.

Governor of the Colony. This was a wise provision; for it was too much to expect of an assemblage of persons taken, many of them, from the lowest condition, and without education, to be able at once to take the whole management of the affairs of a newly established colony. And the successive agents or governors were some of the most wise, disinterested, and noble-minded men that have ever engaged in the founding of a new state. Many of them—as Mills and Ashmun—fell a sacrifice to their ardent devotion to what they justly considered a great and good cause. Monuments will yet be raised to their memory: one to Ashmun, indeed, has already been raised both in America and in Liberia. The founders of this new thing in the world's history, a nation of free and enlightened and Christian Africans will in coming ages find their due place in the regard of mankind: their real reward many of them have already found, we may trust, in a higher sphere.

While, however, the Governor or Head of the colony was to be a white person, the Lieutenant-Governor, Counselors, Judges, Members of the Legislature, and all other officers whatever, were to be men of color. This arrangement continued for a long time, and worked exceedingly well. A few years since, however—after experience had been gained by the colonists in managing public affairs, and it was found that all things were going on with good order and quietness, as well as efficiency—the Society at home resolved to trust them still further; and, on the death of one of the agents,—a colored person, Lieutenant-Governor Roberts, who had already shown much skill and wisdom in conducting affairs, was appointed Governor; and the Society had no reason to repent their choice. And still further, when it was thus found that the colonists could be safely entrusted with the whole management of affairs, the Society generously gave them their independence—the first instance, perhaps, in all history, of so noble and disinterested a public transaction.

The organization of the Republic as an independent State took place in July, 1847. The Constitution is modeled after that of the United States. The Government consists of a President, a Vice-President, with a Senate and House of Representatives, the number of members in the former being six, and in the latter twenty-eight. The first President, elected under the new Constitution, was the former excellent Governor, Mr. Roberts.

In 1848, President Roberts visited Europe, and was received by the Governments of both England and France, which Powers acknowledged the independence of the new Republic, and negotiated with it treaties of commerce. From an article on Liberia, which appeared in the London *Times* about the period of President Roberts's visit, we make the following extract, which presents some interesting particulars:—

"Since its commencement in 1820 [1822], its population, including the aborigines, who have incorporated themselves with the immigrants, has increased to upwards of 80,000, while the land they occupy extends along 320 miles of coast, and reaches on an average about eighty miles into the interior. The proportion of the population born in America, or of American descent, is estimated at about 10,000;* and such has been the effect of their example and influence, that out of the remaining 70,000, consisting of aborigines, and of captives released from slavers, at least 50,000 can speak the English language, so that any one would perfectly understand them; while their habits are rapidly becoming those of civilized and steady agriculturists. The desire for education is also manifested by the surrounding tribes, and instances are not uncommon of natives sending their children four or five hundred miles from the interior to be instructed in the primary schools established in the Republic. Of these there are thirty-six in operation, and an average attendance in each of about forty aboriginal pupils.

"The whole of the territory of Liberia has been purchased from time to time from the aboriginal owners, and in this way at least twenty petty sovereignties have been extinguished. In its former condition, the coast was the constant resort of slaves; but the traffic is now effectually suppressed as far as the jurisdiction of the Republic extends; and its entire

* This number has now increased to upwards of 12,000, and the number of aborigines under the Liberian jurisdiction is estimated at 340,000; while the coast-line, including the late purchase of Gallinas, cannot be less than 700 miles.—See Chambers's *Repository of Instructive and Amusing Tracts*, No. 57, "Liberia."

This Tract presents a brief, but interesting sketch of Liberia, its history and present condition. It appears, from the same Tract, that the Government of Brazil has recently appointed a *Chargé d'Affaires* to Liberia, the Chevalier Miteroi, who, in addition to his ordinary duties, is specially instructed to make preparations for the establishment of a colony of Brazilian free blacks. Hence the return of the Africans from the South, as well as the North, American Continent, may soon be expected to commence.

abandonment is an invariable stipulation in every treaty of trade and protection, into which the Republic may consent to enter with neighboring states. The disposition to avail themselves of treaties of this description is plainly on the increase on the part of the surrounding natives; and it is estimated that not less than 2,000,000 of persons in the interior now obtain their supply of European goods from the Republic, and from the kindred colony of Cape Palmas. Last year, eighty-two foreign vessels visited Liberia, and exchanged merchandise for articles of African production to the amount of 600,000 dollars.

"The natural resources of Liberia are immense, and are steadily in process of development. The climate, although more healthy than Sierra Leone, is still deadly to Europeans; but the improvement it has undergone during the last ten years, from the effect of clearing and drainage, is stated to have been most remarkable. The colored immigrants from America, who used invariably to suffer from fever on their arrival, are now able to go to work at once. The duration of life amongst the colonists is considered to be about the same as in England."

An article in *Chambers's Edinburgh Journal*, published about the same time, thus speaks of the new Republic:

"Liberia is the most interesting colony in existence, and from its history we may draw some useful lessons in social economics. It is a settlement of pure negroes, speaking the English language, imbued with the Anglo-American civilization, and influenced by Christian belief and ethics. Placed on the African coast facing the Atlantic, it may be said to present a cheering spot on that great waste,—a frontier of intelligence to what has been hitherto a wide-spread and hopeless world of savagery. The success of this experiment at colonizing, is in many respects interesting. In the first place, it is, we think, conclusively shown, that the negro races may be impressed with all the ordinary characteristics of a civilized people, and that they are thus capable of that species of self-government which marks a high state of intellectual advancement. Of their capacities for assuming this condition, after due culture and experience in orderly habits, we indeed never entertained a doubt. It is very pleasing to find that out of the rude and unshapely mass of negroism, there has at length arisen a people, who, in the eye of the world, vindicate their claim to humanity, their full and fair title to be treated as men and brothers. It is true that an experiment of the same nature has been less successful in Hayti, greatly to the damage of arguments in favor of negro self-government; and some may fear that the present effort in Liberia may terminate as ingloriously. But the two cases are scarcely parallel. Hayti commenced its career in blood and violence; and its civilization never appears to have been anything but a French polish, beneath which there was neither intellectual culture nor moral or religious restraints. The basis of Liberian independence is very different. The nation was begun in Christian love, was fostered with the parental tenderness of superior intellect, and, attaining strength and self-confidence, has at last been committed to its own experienced guidance. Its civilization, moreover, is essentially Anglo-Saxon; and with the English tongue and the English Bible, not to speak of a spirit of English industry, we may suppose it to possess a power of endurance, and skill in management, which unhappily never distinguished the imperfect nationality of Hayti."*

To the ability, wisdom, and dignified deportment of the gentlemen (for such they truly are, in all respects) who fill the offices of trust and honor in the Liberian Government, we have many testimonials. In reference to President Roberts,—Commodore Perry, of the United States navy, in a report to his Government, dated in 1844, says: "Governors Roberts, of Liberia, and Russworm, of Cape Palmas, are intelligent and estimable men, executing their responsible functions with wisdom and dignity; and we have, in the example of these two gentlemen, irrefragable proof of the capability of colored people to govern themselves." Mr. Buchanan, late Governor of the Pennsylvania Colony at Bassa Cove, in an account of a visit which he made to Monrovia, says, "I also attended their courts, and was gratified to observe the perfect good order and decorum with which the proceedings were conducted; the dignity and good sense of the judges, the shrewdness and legal acumen of the counsel, the patient attention of the jury,—all, of course, colored men."—"It is a highly honorable fact," says Mr. Freeman† (the remark may be quoted in this connection), "that no capital crime has ever been committed in the colony. The crimes usually brought before the court

* *Chambers's Journal* of December 16, 1848.
† *Plea for Africa*, Conversation XXIV.

are thefts committed by natives within the Colonial jurisdiction." There are also Boards of Agriculture, of Public Works, of Health, all the members of which are of course men of color,—and the management of these and other public affairs is conducted with energy and intelligence. Most of the public officers are elected annually by the people.

In reference to the high state of morals in the colony, there is very strong testimony. Governor Mechlin, a former Governor of the colony, remarks,— "As to the morals of the colonists, I consider them much better than those of the people of the United States; that is, you may take an equal number of the inhabitants from any section of the Union, and you will find more drunkenness, more profane swearers and Sabbath-breakers, than in Liberia. You rarely hear an oath; and as to riots and breaches of the peace, I recollect but one instance, and that of a trifling nature, since I assumed the government of the colony." The Rev. Beverly R. Wilson, an intelligent colored minister of the Methodist Episcopal Church, spent fourteen months in Liberia, which he visited, at his own expense, to ascertain whether he could find there an advantageous home for himself and family. He says: "The morals of the colonists I regard as superior to the same population in almost any part of the United States. A drunkard is a rare spectacle, and when exhibited is put under the ban of public opinion at once. To the praise of Liberia be it spoken, I did not hear, during my residence in it, a solitary oath uttered by a settler: this abominable practice has not yet stained its moral character and reputation, and

Heaven grant that it never may. In such detestation is the daily use of ardent spirits held, that two of the towns have already prohibited its sale, or rather confined it to the apothecaries' shops. In Monrovia it is still viewed as an article of traffic and merchandise, but it is destined there to share the same fate. The Temperance Society is in full operation, and will soon root it out. The Sabbath is rigidly observed and respected: but few cases of disorder occur, and they are confined to the baser sorts, a few of which infest Liberia. Religion and all its institutions are greatly respected; in fact, a decided majority are religionists, and by their pious demeanor are exerting a very salutary influence, not only upon the emigrants, but also upon the natives, among whom a door is opened for the propagation of Christianity." Mr. Wilson, addressing himself to the colored people in the United States, concludes by saying, "If you desire liberty, surely Liberia holds out great and distinguished inducements. Here you can never be free; but there, living under the administration of the laws enacted by yourselves, you may enjoy that freedom, which in the very nature of things you cannot experience in this country:—

"Liberia, happy land! thy shore
Entices with a thousand charms;
And calls—his wonted thraldom o'er—
Her ancient exile to her arms.

"Come hither, son of Afric, come;
And o'er the wide and weltering sea,
Behold thy lost and lovely home,
That fondly waits to welcome thee." *

In regard to the state of education in Liberia,—we

* *Plea for Africa*, Conversation XXIV.

have already seen, from the article in the London *Times*, that there are no fewer than thirty-six primary schools. The author of the *Plea for Africa*, writing in 1837, remarks: "The subject of education has ever been one of primary importance with the Board of Colonization. In 1830, the Board established permanent schools in the towns of Monrovia, Caldwell, and Millsburgh. They adopted a thorough system of instruction, which is now in successful operation. There are two female schools, conducted on liberal principles, one of which was established by a lady in Philadelphia, who sent out the necessary books and teachers. It is said, *there is not a child or youth in the colony but is provided with an appropriate school.* Some of these schools have valuable libraries. There is a public library at Monrovia, which contains between 1,200 and 2,000 volumes. A printing press is in operation there, issuing a weekly and well-conducted gazette, the *Liberia Herald.* It is interesting to look over this sheet, and see the various advertisements, notices of auctions, parades, marriages—together with its marine list—as if the print were issued from the midst of an old and long established community." In addition to the numerous common schools, a plan was some years ago set on foot (and, we trust, carried into operation) by the American Society 'for the promotion of Education in Africa,' for establishing a college in Liberia, where all the higher branches of learning might be taught, and where young men might be fitted for the liberal professions.*

* From Chambers's *Tract*, before referred to, we learn, that in 1851 there were three High Schools in Monrovia; and in 1852 an act was passed incorporating a board of Trustees for a College.

Lastly, in reference to the state of *Religion* in Liberia, it is interesting to see how early and how deeply the religious spirit seemed to influence the colonists, giving to the "Pilgrims of Mesurado" (as they have been called), as it did to the Pilgrim Fathers of New England, their strength and power of endurance, their wisdom, and their final prosperity. "The cause of religion in the colony," says Mr. Freeman, "seems always to have been an object of much solicitude on the part of the Colonization Society. The churches are generally well supplied with respectable and faithful ministers. In all these churches there are Sunday schools established, to which the most promising young people in the colony have attached themselves either as teachers or as scholars. I have," he says, "in a pamphlet before me, printed in Monrovia, the 'Minutes of the first Convention of the Liberia Baptist Association,' by which it appears that there are in the colony six Baptist churches, comprising about 220 members. These 'Minutes' represent the Baptist churches as in a flourishing condition; and the proceedings of the Convention, and their circular to the churches, evince talent, judgment, and piety, of a very respectable order. Here is an extract from their 'Minutes':

"'Princes shall come out of Egypt, Ethiopia shall soon stretch out her hands unto God'—is the prediction of a holy prophet, uttered ages antecedent to the advent of the Messiah. And when we reflect on the midnight darkness which, from time immemorial, has shrouded this portion of Africa, we hail with rapture the first dawning of that glorious gospel-day, which is signified in this oracle. He with whom a thousand years is as a day, and a day as a thousand years, works his own sovereign will, and effects his own purposes of grace and goodness, in a manner above the comprehension of men. For ages Africa has been 'meted out, and trodden down.' Her deep moral degradation seems, by universal consent, to have been justification in regarding her as lawful plunder, and as a land on which a curse rests. But we rejoice that these days are going by. The darkness of ages is yielding to the bright rising of the 'Sun of Righteousness.' Idolatry and superstition are retiring before Christianity and civilization; and on the mountain-top, once defiled by sacrifices to devils, the banner of the cross is unfurled, while a voice in the wilderness is proclaiming, '*The kingdom of heaven is at hand.*'"

This is certainly an eloquent passage; and when we think of its having been written by men who, or whose fathers, were once degraded African slaves, our admiration is greatly increased.

"I have here, also," continues Mr. Freeman, "the 'Report of the Liberia Mission of the Methodist Episcopal Church, and the Minutes of their Annual Conference in Liberia in 1835.' This document is full of interest, and displays the same zeal, energy, and ability which you find generally among the colonists. Of the Conference the Report says: 'The greatest harmony and peace prevailed during our session; and it is confidently hoped that this little band of ambassadors of Christ have gone to their respective appointments with increasing zeal in the cause of their Divine Master, and holy resolutions to spend and be spent in the blessed work of winning souls to God.'—It would seem from the Minutes, that the number of ministers of their denomination in the colony, in 1835, was twelve, and the number of communicants upwards of 200. The Report also speaks of the appointment of a 'Missionary for the interior of Africa, to carry the light of the Gospel of Jesus Christ into the dark regions of this benighted land.' The appointment, it is stated, seems to be regarded by the members of the Conference with the warmest approbation; and one good result already discovered from it is the awakening of a missionary spirit among the preachers. Several are ready to say, 'Here we are, send us. We covet the privilege of carrying the Gospel to the heathen tribes.' The Report concludes: 'If we are to judge from the appearance of the fields around us, which are already white unto harvest, we should conclude that "the set time to favor Zion has come," yea, that "*now* is the accepted time, now is the day of salvation." Men and brethren, help! O help to disenthral poor Africa from the hellish grasp of the enemy of all righteousness! Help to promote the moral and religious prosperity of this infant colony, destined as it is to be rendered "a savor of life unto life" to this benighted continent.'"*

In a number of the *Liberia Herald*, a newspaper published at Monrovia, is an interesting account of the formation of a body of native Africans, thirty-six in number, into a Christian church. The article, as quoted by Mr. Freeman, reads as follows:—

"On Sunday, the 7th inst., thirty-six native Afri-

---

* *Plea for Africa*, Conversation XXIV.

cans, resident at New Georgia, late members of the first Baptist Church in this place [Monrovia], having been dismissed by letters, were brought into visibility as a Church, in the place of their residence. Sermon by Rev. Dr. Skinner,—charge and right hand of fellowship by Rev. H. Teage, and concluding prayer by Rev. A. W. Anderson. The exercises of the occasion were truly solemnly pleasing and impressive. They naturally threw the mind back to the period, when they who were thus solemnly dedicating themselves to God, to be constituted into a 'golden candlestick,' from which the Divine light is to chase the surrounding gloom, were themselves in the darkness of nature, without God, without revelation, and consequently without the hope it inspires."

Here, truly, is fruit; here is success; here is effective missionary action. Not often can such results of missionary labors be shown. In truth, Africa is the grandest missionary field in the world: but colored men, Africans themselves, must be the missionaries.

Here follows another item from the same paper. It is a communication from a correspondent of the *Herald*, in Monrovia, and relates to the dedication of a Presbyterian Church:

"Mr. Editor, as every circumstance which has any relation to the spreading of our blessed religion in Africa, must have a tendency to give satisfaction to every lover and follower of the religion of Jesus Christ —you will confer a favor on one of your constant readers by giving publication to this. Having understood that the First Presbyterian Church was to be dedicated to the service of God on the 26th of November, I attended, and was happy to find the principal part of the inhabitants of this town present on so interesting an occasion. Every denomination of saints seemed to rejoice that another temple had been erected and dedicated to the worship of Almighty God. It was enough that the pure religion of Jesus Christ was to be inculcated from that sacred pulpit, and as that servant of God, the Rev. C. Teage, remarked, 'where he then stood, preaching the dedication sermon, sixteen years ago, the devil's bush stood.'—How truly animating it is to see temples arise for the worship of God, where not long since there was nothing to be heard, but the savage yell of the native, or the clanking of the poor slaves' chains!"

We have thus given a sketch of the physical and moral condition of Liberia. We have dwelt upon it, in some detail, because we consider it, in the language of the writer in *Chambers's Journal*, "the most interesting colony in existence,"— because we fully agree with the declaration of the enlightened and far-seeing British nobleman, who pronounced the foundation of the Colony of Liberia, "one of the greatest events of modern times:"* and still further, because we hold it to be the key to that problem we have undertaken to solve,—the reason for the permission, by Divine Providence, of the African slave-trade and slavery in the New World. Without this key, all is dark: with it, all is light; and through the door which that key opens, we behold a vista extending far into the regions of futurity, through which we discern in the distance two continents, America and Africa, freed, purified,

* See p. 64.

and happy,—blessed, both of them, with liberty, Christianity, and peace.

But how, it will be asked, is that great result to be brought about through so insignificant an instrumentality as that of the Colony of Liberia, a little State, composed of a few emigrant blacks? Ha! when the wise and knowing king James saw a small vessel, the "Mayflower," push off from the English coast, with a little band of emigrants, fleeing from religious persecution, and bound to the shores of the new western World,—what idea had he, think you, that, led on by Providence, they were going to lay the foundation of a great nation, which would one day extend itself across that continent, from ocean to ocean, and which would at length powerfully influence the destinies of the world? But the prophetic eye reads effects in causes: in the shooting acorn it sees the mighty oak; in the first drooping branch of the Banyan-tree, it perceives a future forest; in Adam and Eve, it beholds a populous world. Show the reflective man but a *principle*, and he will give you a thousand results, which to the common mind are indiscernible till they are actually produced: from a single fossil bone, a Cuvier will present you the whole form of the animal to which it belonged, tell you its habits and history, and draw you a sketch of the country and scenery through which it roamed.

SECTION V.

DISTINCT CHARACTER OF THE COLORED RACE—WHY THE AFRICAN SLAVE-TRADE HAS BEEN PERMITTED—EMIGRATION OF THE FREE BLACKS TO LIBERIA.

FROM the authentic and satisfactory accounts which we have of Liberia—some particulars of which have been adduced in the preceding pages—we draw the conclusion, that it is the true home and country for the free, intelligent, and Christianized colored man: and that in laboring to make it such a home, the hand of Providence is distinctly visible, in the whole history of its foundation and progress. That is enough: all the other conclusions follow from this as a premise: both the deliverance of America and the regeneration of Africa are the necessary consequences: it remains but a question of time. *Potens est veritas, et prevalebit:* —" Truth is mighty and will prevail." In spite of opposition and obloquy, in spite of indifference and contempt, the cause of African Colonization will at length, we believe, completely triumph. The free blacks of the United States, will at length discover their true interests, will at length perceive that if they would consult their own real happiness, and the lasting good, moral and physical, of themselves and their children—if, in a word, they would become truly freemen, not only legally, but civilly and socially, they must separate themselves from the whites, and go where they will be in a community of their own color and kin, and where they will be on perfectly equal terms with all around them. It requires but little thought to show them this: in fact, they know it already and feel it. The nobler-spirited of them feel deeply their state of humiliation, and the more intelligent of them begin to perceive the only remedy for it. Africa, the home of their fathers, calls to them across the sea, and spreads her arms to welcome them. Here, she says, is all you wish; here is a home, freedom, and happiness. Here the colored man is in dignity and in power. Here are no whites to frown upon you, to pass you by with disregard, to oppress or disturb you. Here you may be not only a voter, an elector, but also yourself eligible to the highest offices. Here you may be a member of the Legislature, a Judge, the Vice-President, the President himself, if you but possess the capacity and fitness. All places of honor and trust are open to you. All the professions, too, are free to you: here, the lawyer, the physician, the clergyman are all colored men, like yourselves, yet loved, esteemed, and honored, looked up to for counsel and instruction, in all concerns, whether affecting the body or the soul, whether temporal or eternal. Here, too, the avenues to wealth are all open. The merchant, the ship-owner, the land-holder, are here all men of color, yet possessing weight and influence in the community—gentlemen, respectable, and respected by all. Here everything is in abundance; comforts and luxuries invite you on every side. You may literally "sit under your own vine and fig-tree, with none to make you afraid." In the soft evening-hour, after the duties of the day are over, you may sit at the door of your own mansion, and while the cool sea-breeze is breathing upon you, and the new moon is hanging in beauty over the western waters, you will look across that ocean, and—thinking of the land of the whites that lies beyond—you will bless the day you left it, to come to the home of your fathers, the rich country which Providence has set apart for the colored race.

While Africa is thus calling them, America is urging them away. Their presence is not desired by the whites; they are felt to be a foreign element in the body politic, one that cannot amalgamate with its system,—one, the removal of which is necessary to its safety, health, and peace. This feeling is founded, doubtless, on the intrinsic distinction between the two races, which the Creator himself has marked. That Creator has divided mankind into distinct races; not two only, but many. At least five distinct races are, as we know, universally recognized by ethnographers,—namely, the yellow or Asiatic race, the brown or Malays, the copper-colored or American-Indian, the negro or African, and the Caucasian or white race. The mixture of any two of these has not in general been found to be for the advantage of either party. There are fundamental differences between them, not only in physical, but in mental constitution. Mixed races, it has been generally found, are degenerate races.

This being the case, it is evident that the repugnance

felt by the whites at the idea of intermixture with the African race, is not without a foundation in something real,—in a feeling implanted, doubtless, for the very purpose of keeping the races distinct. Nor is this feeling by any means confined, in its direction, to the African race alone. Would there not be felt the same or a greater abhorrence at the idea of intermarriage with an American-Indian,—with a Malay,—with a Chinese? Thus, we perceive, on a little reflection, that it is not a sentiment confined, in its direction, to the Africans. Nor is the existence of such a feeling by any means exclusively to be found with *American* whites, as has sometimes been unjustly charged. It exists with whites of all nations, who have been brought to any considerable extent into contact with the African race. It is found with people of all the different nations that possess the several West India islands—the English, French, Spanish, Swedes, Danes. All these have a similar repugnance to an amalgamation with the negro. There may be a slight difference in the degree of this feeling—the French and Spanish, perhaps, manifesting less of it than the others: but, of all the whites, the Anglo-Saxon race, whether the English in the West Indies, or the Americans in the United States, are most deeply imbued with it. In England itself, indeed, the feeling can scarcely be said to exist; and simply for the reason that there being few or no negroes in that country, there has been no opportunity for its exercise—nothing to call it forth or to produce it.*

* Says the late Mr. Kinmont (a Scotchman long resident in America, and a very able and original writer), "An example of the evil resulting

But because the African race is distinct from the white, does it follow that it is *inferior?* By no means. That is a point not proved; nor has the day for fair comparison yet arrived. But even if it should appear that the white is superior in intellectual capacity, yet it is certain that the African is the superior in the nobler part of man—the *heart.* It is the testimony of Mungo Park, and of other travelers in Africa, that the negroes, even in their present uncultivated state, are a gentle, feeling, affectionate race. How many touching

from mixing science with religion, to the injury of both, may be seen in the argument for the amalgamation of the African and European races, on the ground of their being one family, both descended from Adam and Eve. It belongs to science and to the common instincts and feelings of mankind to say, whether there are not races of men, so unlike in their temperaments as to prohibit, as nefarious and contrary to nature, the amalgamation of them. The identity and unity of the human family, imaged in Adam and Eve, is a religious, not a scientific truth; and any deductions made from it, to have any presumption of fairness, must be religious, not scientific. Thus, if from the unity of the human family, so acknowledged, it be argued that we owe to every race of mankind on the globe the same obligations of justice and mercy which we owe to each other, the argument would be a good one, and would brand those horrid acts of injustice of which the white race have been guilty, both to the black and to the red. But it may be safely affirmed, that had it not been for the debasement of the moral sense, the result of such injustice, the natural repugnance to amalgamation among these races, particularly between the black and the white, would have been such, that it could never have taken place under any circumstances. But men having first lost all sense of shame, in destroying the natural birth-right of freedom in a distinct branch of the human family, no wonder this second curse—an unnatural confusion of races—has followed on the back of the other, and that we should be about to incur this sad penalty of the transgression of the natural laws of justice and humanity. The Copts, or modern Egyptians, are a mixed race of Negroes and Caucasians, and hence their degradation."—*Twelve Lectures on the Natural History of Man,* p. 152, by Alex. Kinmont, A.M., Cincinnati, 1838.

instances does Park relate of their kindness to him, while wandering in the wilds of the African continent!*

* One of these we cannot forbear extracting. Park, after escaping from the Moors, had reached Sego, the capital of the kingdom of Bambarra, where for the first time he saw the long looked-for river Niger. The king, on hearing of Park's arrival, forbade his crossing the river to visit him—probably with the well-meant purpose of keeping him out of the hands of his enemies, the Moors, who were numerous in that capital. He was thus left in a very uncomfortable situation. "I was regarded," he says, "with astonishment and fear, and was obliged to sit all day without victuals under the shade of a tree; and the night threatened to be very uncomfortable, for the wind arose, and there was great appearance of a heavy rain; and the wild beasts are so very numerous in this neighborhood, that I should have been under the necessity of climbing up the tree, and resting amongst the branches. About sunset, however, as I was preparing to spend the night in this manner, and had turned my horse loose that he might graze at liberty,—a woman, returning from the labors of the field, stopped to observe me, and, perceiving that I was weary and dejected, inquired into my situation, which I briefly explained to her; whereupon, with looks of great compassion, she took up my saddle and bridle, and told me to follow her. Having conducted me into her hut, she lighted a lamp, spread a mat on the floor, and told me I might remain there for the night. Finding that I was very hungry, she said she would procure me something to eat. She accordingly went out, and returned in a short time with a very fine fish, which, having caused to be half broiled upon some embers, she gave me for supper. The rites of hospitality being thus performed towards a stranger in distress, my worthy benefactress (pointing to the mat, and telling me I might sleep there without apprehension), called to the female part of the family, who had stood gazing on me all the while in fixed astonishment, to resume their task of spinning cotton, in which they continued to employ themselves a great part of the night. They lightened their labor with songs, one of which was composed extempore, for I was myself the subject of it. It was sung by one of the young women, the rest joining in a sort of chorus. The air was sweet and plaintive; and the words literally translated were these:—' The winds roared and the rains fell. The poor white man, faint and weary, came and sat under our tree. He has no mother to bring him milk, no wife to grind his corn. *Chorus.*—Let us pity the white man,—no mother

It is quite possible, as has been remarked by the intelligent writer already quoted (Mr. Kinmont), that the African race is yet destined to show to the world a new and loftier species of civilization than has yet been seen,—not the cold and hard civilization of cultivated intellect merely, but the heavenly civilization of goodness, peace, and mutual love. "There can be no question," he says, "that when the epoch of their civilization arrives, in the lapse of ages, they will display in their native land some very peculiar and interesting traits of character, of which we, a distinct branch of the human family, can at present form no conception. It will be—indeed, it must be—a civilization of a peculiar stamp; perhaps we might venture to conjecture, not so much distinguished by art, as a certain beautiful nature,—not so marked or adorned by science, as exalted and refined by a certain new and lovely theology;—a reflection of the light of heaven, more perfect and endearing than

has he,' &c.—Trifling as this recital may appear to the reader, to a person in my situation the circumstance was affecting in the highest degree."—Park's *Travels in the Interior of Africa*, chap. 15.

How beautiful, too, was the conduct of the king of Boussa to the Landers, while on their way down the Niger, to discover its outlet! "The king of Boussa," says the narrative, "sent messengers down the Niger, to a town called Rabba, in order to pave the way for the secure passage of the travelers. When a favorable answer was returned, the African monarch *capered round his hut* with transport; and after a burst of joy, he began to cry like a child—his heart was so full. 'Now,' said he, 'whatever may happen to the white men, my neighbors cannot but acknowledge that I have taken every care of them, treated them as became a king, and done my best to promote their happiness and interests.' And so he has," continue the Landers.—What a picture of goodness is this! The civilized monarchs of Europe may well take a lesson from it.

that which the intellects of the Caucasian race have ever yet exhibited. There is more of the *child*, of unsophisticated nature, in the Negro race than in the European,— a circumstance, however, which must always lower them in the estimation of a people whose natural distinction is a manly and proud bearing, and an extreme proneness to artificial society and social institutions. If the Caucasian race is destined, as would appear from the precocity of their genius, and their natural quickness, and extreme aptitude to the arts, to reflect the lustre of the Divine *wisdom*, or, to speak more properly, of *science*,—shall we envy the Negro, if a later but far nobler civilization await him, —to return the splendor of the Divine attributes of *mercy and benevolence*, in the practice and exhibition of all the milder and gentler virtues? It is true, the present rude lineaments of the race might seem to give little warrant for the indulgence of hopes so romantic; but yet those who will reflect upon the natural constitution of the African may see some ground even for such anticipations. Can we not read an aptitude for this species of civilization I refer to, in that singular light-heartedness which distinguishes the whole race,—in their natural want of solicitude about the future—in them a vice at present, but yet the natural basis of a virtue—and, especially, in that natural talent for music with which they are pre-eminently endowed;—to say nothing of that willingness to *serve*, the most beautiful trait of humanity, which we, from our innate love of dominion, and in defiance of the Christian religion, brand with the name of *servility*, and abuse, not less to our own dishonor than to their injury. But even amid these untoward circumstances, there burst forth occasionally the indications of that better destiny, to which nature herself will at last conduct them."* We think there is much probability in this view. And the course of the Liberian colony thus far is proof of it. Where is there, on record, an account of a colony or settlement of whites, taken from among a class so degraded and uneducated as that from which many of the Liberians were drawn—who conducted themselves so well, so admirably with so much order, propriety, and harmony? We may safely say there never has been such a colony. Nor, moreover, have the Liberians shown any want of energy or ability. And it yet remains to be seen whether they will not manifest by and by, intellectual capacities equal to those of the white race.†

* Kinmont's *Lectures*, pp. 190, 191.

† Mr. Freeman, in his *Plea for Africa*, has collected many instances of distinguished blacks—eminent in literature, science, and even in the military art. Among these are the following: "J. E. J. CAPITEIN, born in Africa, and bought by a slave-holder, on the river St. Andre, was carried to Holland, where he acquired a knowledge of Latin, Greek, Hebrew, and Chaldaic. He studied theology at the University of Leyden, took his degree, was ordained at Amsterdam, and went out as a missionary to Guinea, in 1742. He was the author of several published sermons, poems, and dissertations. His *Dissertatio de Servitute Libertati Christianæ non contraria*, went through four editions. A. W. Amo, born in Guinea, was brought to this country when young, took the degree of Doctor of Philosophy, at the University of Wittemberg, in 1734. He was skilled in Latin and Greek, and delivered lectures on philosophy; in 1744, he supported a thesis at Wittemberg, and published a dissertation *On the Absence of Sensation in the Soul, and its Presence in the Human Body*; was appointed Professor, and the same year supported a thesis 'On the Distinction which ought to be made between the

It is not therefore, we would repeat, on the ground of any intrinsic inferiority in the African race, that we think they should be separated from the whites, but

Operations of Mind and those of Sense.' He also distinguished himself in mathematics. In an account of his life published by the Academic Council, his integrity, talents, industry, and erudition are very highly commended. FRANCIS WILLIAMS, a negro, born in Jamaica, was educated in the University of Cambridge, England: he opened a school in Jamaica for instruction in Latin and mathematics, and wrote many pieces in Latin verse, which discovered talents of a good order. PHILLIS WHEATLEY, who was born in Africa, torn from her country at the age of seven, and in 1761 sold to John Wheatley, of Boston, United States. Allowed to employ herself in study, she rapidly attained a knowledge of the Latin language. In 1772, at the age of nineteen, and still a slave, she published a volume of religious and moral poetry, which passed through several editions on both sides the Atlantic. She obtained her freedom in 1775, and died five years afterwards. THOMAS FULLER, a native African, resident for some time near Alexandria, in the District of Columbia, although unable to read or write, was an extraordinary example of quickness in reckoning. Being asked, in company, for the purpose of trying his powers, how many seconds a person had lived who was seventy years, seven months, and seven days old,—he answered correctly in a minute and a-half. On reckoning it up after him, a different result was obtained by the company. 'Have you not forgotten the leap years?' said the negro. These they had forgotten: the omission being supplied, the answer was found to be right. This account was given by Dr. Rush, when Fuller was seventy years old. BENJAMIN BANNAKER, a negro of Maryland, applied himself to Astronomy with so much success that he published almanacs in Philadelphia for the years 1794 and 1795. JAMES DERHAM was once a slave in Philadelphia. In 1788, at the age of twenty-one, he became the most distinguished physician in New Orleans. 'I conversed with him on medicine,' says Dr. Rush, 'and found him very learned; I thought I could give him information concerning the treatment of diseases, but I learned more from him than he could expect from me.' Boerhasve and De Haen have given strong testimony to the medical skill of not a few blacks. Several are mentioned as having been very dexterous surgeons. JOSEPH RACHEL, a free negro of Barbadoes, was another *Howard*. Having become rich by commerce, he devoted all his property to charitable because we believe it to be the manifest order of nature and intention of Divine Providence. And the blacks should be as unwilling to ally themselves with the white race, as the whites with them: they should feel the same repugnance to it; and this they probably would feel, but for the fact of their having been so long in an inferior situation, and therefore accustomed to look up to the whites as a superior class. In their native Africa, they certainly do entertain a similar repugnance to the whites. Park testifies that it was manifested towards him by many of the negroes. The African belles (and he describes some of them) thought him diseased and deformed, and would probably have felt the same repugnance at the idea of intermarriage with him, as the white ladies naturally do at that of a

uses, and spent much of his time in visiting prisons to relieve and reclaim the wretched tenants. He died in 1758. HANNIBAL, an African negro, rose to the rank of Lieutenant-General and Director of Artillery, under Peter the Great, of Russia. His son was also Lieutenant-General in the Russian corps of Artillery. [We may add to these the name of TOUSSAINT L'OUVERTURE, General and afterwards Governor of the negroes of St. Domingo, who, for his patriotism and excellence of character, as well as for his military skill and political wisdom, may almost be denominated the *Washington* of negroes.] Professor Blumenbach," continues Mr. Freeman, "possessed a library composed entirely of works written by negroes. He says, there is not a single department of taste or science, in which these people have not been distinguished. Dr. Blumenbach is the author of the most able and scientific Treatise on the varieties of the human species, and was better qualified than any other person, to decide upon their constitutional differences. He observes that there is no savage people, which have distinguished themselves by such examples of perfectibility and capacity for scientific cultivation; and, consequently, that none can approach more nearly to the polished nations of the globe than the negro."—*Plea for Africa*, pp. 17, 46, second edition.

union with a negro.* The two races are essentially distinct, and that is quite enough to produce the sentiment referred to, without the supposition of intrinsic inferiority on either side. It would certainly be a more manly and dignified course for the intelligent free blacks in America to take this view of the subject, and act accordingly, than to degrade themselves by servilely courting the society of the whites, content to be received among them on terms of mere sufferance.

"But we claim the right," they may say, " to remain in America: it is the place of our birth, and therefore our proper and legitimate home." Grant the right: yet does it follow that it is the wisest course, under present circumstances, to use it? "All things," says the Apostle, "are lawful for me; but all things are not expedient." Where is the wisdom of contending for a barren right—when a voluntary abandonment of it would bring to the holder far greater ease,

* Says Park, "I had no sooner entered the court appropriated to the ladies, than the whole seraglio surrounded me. They were ten or twelve in number, most of them young and handsome, and wearing on their heads ornaments of gold and beads of amber. They rallied me, with a good deal of gaiety, on different subjects, particularly on the whiteness of my skin and the prominency of my nose. They insisted that both were artificial. The first, they said, was produced when I was an infant, by dipping me in milk; and they insisted that my nose had been pinched every day, till it had acquired its present unsightly and unnatural conformation. On my part, without denying my own deformity, I paid them many compliments on African beauty: I praised the glossy jet of their skins, and the lovely depression of their noses. But they said that flattery or (as they emphatically termed it) *honey-mouth*, was not esteemed in Bornou. In return, however, for my company or compliments (to which, by the way, they seemed not so insensible as they affected to be) they presented me with a jar of honey and some fish, which were sent to my lodgings."—Park's *Travels*, chap. iv.

peace, and self-respect? "You will tell me," says the chivalrous George Harris, in his letter to his colored friends, "that our race have equal right to mingle in the American republic, as the Irishman, the German, the Swede. Granted, they have. But then, *I do not want it;* I want a country, a nation of my own. I think that the African race has peculiarities yet to be unfolded, in the light of civilization and Christianity, which if not the same with those of the Anglo-Saxon, may prove to be morally of even a higher type. To the Anglo-Saxon race have been entrusted the destinies of the world during its pioneer period of struggle and conflict. To that mission, its stern, inflexible, energetic elements were well adapted; but as a Christian, I look for another era to arise. On its borders I trust we stand; and the throes that now convulse the nations are, to my hope, but the birth-pangs of an hour of universal peace and brotherhood. I trust that the development of Africa is to be essentially a Christian one. If not a dominant and commanding race, they are, at least, an affectionate, magnanimous, and forgiving one. Having been schooled in the furnace of injustice and oppression, they have need to bind closer to their hearts that sublime doctrine of love and forgiveness through which alone they are to conquer, and which it is to be their mission to spread over the continent of Africa.—As a Christian patriot, as a teacher of Christianity, I go to *my country*, my chosen, my glorious Africa: and to her, in my heart, I sometimes apply those splendid words of prophecy, 'Whereas thou hast been forsaken and hated, so that no man went through thee, I will make thee an eternal excellence, a joy of many generations.'"*

Observe that in this process of separation, which is already begun and must finally be consummated, between the two races, it is not the blacks, in all cases, that will have to withdraw. In the West Indies, it is the whites, rather, that are removing; and this will probably continue, and to a still greater extent. This is the case especially in the English West India Islands. According to a report, made to the Assembly of Jamaica in January, 1853—there had been, since 1848, a total abandonment of no fewer than one hundred and twenty-eight coffee estates, and a partial abandonment of seventy-one; also, an entire abandonment of ninety-six sugar estates, and a partial abandonment of sixty-six. This course of things, though exceedingly mortifying and distressing to the whites, may be in accordance with the purposes of Divine Providence in reference to those Islands, and will, we hope, result in final good. From the large island of Hayti or St. Domingo, formerly a French colony, the whites have, we know, been driven by force; and it is now altogether in the possession of the blacks. In Jamaica and the other English West India Islands, such a measure, we trust, will never need to be resorted to; the blacks having now been emancipated, the whites will, in all probability, be found gradually and voluntarily to withdraw. This process seems already to have begun. It is the natural order of things, that those should possess who can occupy and use. The negro race is fitted by nature to live and labor in the torrid zone, the tropical

* *Uncle Tom's Cabin*, chap. xliii.

heats of which are intolerable to the whites. Consequently, we conceive it to be *one* of the two great purposes of Providence, in permitting the removal of a portion of the African race to the New World,—to people the torrid zone of that continent and the neighboring islands, with a race capable of cultivating and enjoying it. For it is the will of the good Creator that all parts of the beautiful world He has made, should be filled with happy inhabitants. Now, it is plain that that removal had to be effected, in a manner, by force; for from their ignorance of the maritime art, as well as from other causes, it is manifest that the Africans would never have migrated of themselves. Hence, the temporary permission of the slave-trade, in which, though so distressing in itself, we can yet see the hand of a wise Providence, turning even man's selfishness and hard-heartedness to final good,—

> "Thus, out of evil still educing good,
> And better thence again, and better still,
> In infinite progression." *

Through this instrumentality, moreover,—distressing

* It will be observed that, according to the testimony of Park, a large portion of those taken from Africa had been already slaves from their birth. In the vessel, for instance, in which Park himself sailed, on his return from his first journey—out of one hundred and thirty slaves on board, only about twenty-five had been of free condition: the remaining hundred and five, or more than four-fifths of the whole number, had previously been slaves in Africa. Thus, as far as concerns these, at least, it was little more than a removal from slavery in one country to slavery in another. In this view, the dealings of Providence in regard to them, in permitting their exile, will appear less hard; and when at the same time we take into consideration the important uses which that removal was to effect, that permission will appear plainly intended for wise and merciful ends.

as it was in itself, thousands, and tens of thousands, have been brought out of the darkness of heathenism to a knowledge of the true God and Savior. Among the slaves of the United States, for instance, it is stated by Dr. Baird,* that there are no fewer than 300,000 church members—one-tenth of the whole number, children included (a larger proportion of religious professors, we suspect, than would be found in most countries of Christian Europe); and in the State of South Carolina alone, as stated by Mr. Freeman, there are upwards of 40,000 communicants belonging to the slave population.† Is not here manifest the hand of Divine Goodness and Wisdom, bringing light out of darkness and peace out of pain?‡

---

* *The Progress and Prospects of Christianity in the United States, with Remarks on Slavery in America*, p. 33. By R. Baird, D.D, London, 1851. This Pamphlet contains some very just observations on the subject of slavery.

† *Plea*, Conversation XVI

‡ Much misconception has prevailed in reference to the religious condition of the slaves, in the United States. "I have before me," says Mr. Freeman, "a letter from Georgia, written by a distinguished gentleman to his friend, on this subject. 'With regard to your inquiries,' he says, 'about the religious instruction of the negroes at the south, I would state, that while there is far less interest on this subject among slave-holders than there should be, still we have much reason to be grateful for what is doing, and for what in prospect may be done.—I visited Bryan County, Georgia, a few weeks since, for the exclusive purpose of seeing what was doing there for the negroes.—On one plantation, there is a chapel, where the master meets the adults every night at the ringing of the bell. Reading a portion of Scripture, and explaining it, with singing and prayer, constitute the regular exercises of every night in the week. On the Sabbath they have different and more protracted exercises. A day-school is taught by two young ladies—embracing all the children under twelve or fifteen years of age. The instruction in this and other schools in the county

When, however, the end for which the African slave-trade had been for a time permitted, was sufficiently attained, then, in the Divine Providence, influences were brought to bear upon the evil instrument itself, to check its action. The world became enlightened to see the wrong of that trade, as it had not before seen; the voice of benevolent individuals and of societies was raised against it, and the power of nations was invoked to put a stop to it. The face of the world has now been set against it, and it must ere long cease. But, what is remarkable, the most effective, and probably the only completely

is oral, of course, but it is gratifying to see how great an amount of knowledge the children had acquired in a few months. A Presbyterian minister of Philadelphia was with me, and he said, in unqualified terms, that he had visited no infant schools at the north, better conducted.—A large portion of the wealthy planters either have already built, or contemplate building, churches on their premises, and employing chaplains to preach to their slaves. Ministers of all denominations begin to awake to their duty and responsibility on this subject. Many of them are now devoting themselves *wholly* to this portion of our community.' —' Our clergy,' says another letter (from South Carolina), ' generally pay a particular attention to the black congregations. Many of them give the entire afternoon of the Sabbath to them. Sunday-schools amongst them are almost universally organized. It is also well known that, in religious families, the instruction of the slaves is an object of general solicitude. It is by no means unusual for individual planters, or for two or more in connection, to support a chaplain for the exclusive benefit of their colored people.' "—*Plea*, Conversation XVI.

"I know of no slave-holding state in the Union," remarks Dr. Baird, "where we cannot preach the Gospel to slaves. In several states (not all), laws were made, twenty-five years ago, forbidding to teach the slaves to *read:* this was done solely through fear lest incendiary publications might be, as was madly attempted, circulated among them, to excite them to rise and destroy their masters. But no law has been made to prevent the *preaching* of the Gospel."—*Prospects of Christianity in the United States*, p. 34.

effective, means for putting a stop to that trade, is the return of the exiled Africans themselves (or a large portion of them), civilized and Christianized, to their native shore, and so settling the coast with an enlightened population. Thus wonderful are the workings of Divine Providence. He makes the evil the instrument of its own repression:—He makes the disease its own cure, after it has performed the good work of purging and purifying the system. The Africans, carried away in suffering and distress from a land which, though their native country, and therefore dear to them, was nevertheless itself a land of darkness and wide-spread slavery, return at length —they or their descendants—free, enlightened, spiritualized, to break the shackles of their kindred, to proclaim liberty and light throughout the country of their ancestors; to "give light to them that sit in darkness and the shadow of death,"—"to let the oppressed go free." And while doing this good work, they turn at the same time to the slave-trader, and say with a stern look, "Come no more here—your work is done, your day is past: you need carry away no more of our people to be either re-enslaved or enlightened in a foreign land: light and liberty are brought now to our own doors: we can stay at home and have the blessing of Christianity besides: go! let us see your face no more."*

* "Cape Mesurado was an extensive slave-market, before the settlement of Monrovia. Two thousand slaves were exported annually from the single points of Cape Mesurado and Cape Mount. In 1834, before the settlement of the Pennsylvania Colony at Bassa Cove, 500 slaves were shipped from that place in a single month. 'Wherever the influence of the colony extends,' says a British naval officer, 'the

Who will not join in this noble enterprise? What enlightened and high-souled free colored man in America will not come forward and give his aid to this cause, when he once understands it, and sees its grand bearings? Here the work is entirely your own; the white man cannot take part in it, except by sympathy or pecuniary aid—he cannot personally join in this holy crusade against the Powers of Darkness and of African bondage: that climate is his grave— God made it so, but He has made it your healthy and happy home. For He was determined that the gentle African should have a land—and a noble land, too— which the restless white man should not intrude upon, but at the expense of life.† Come, then (we would say to the free colored man of America), come and join in this high enterprise which God has committed to you; become His instruments in carrying out the great purpose which the Divine Providence had in view in

slave-trade has been abandoned by the natives, and the peaceable fruits of legitimate commerce established in its place.' Twenty or thirty colonies scattered along the coast would probably put an end to the trade effectually and for ever."—Freeman's *Plea*.

† It is astonishing to observe how many white men have met their death in attempting to explore Africa. First, the distinguished American traveler, Ledyard—whom Park calls his "predecessor"—who died in Egypt at the commencement of his African career. (See Sparks's *Life of Ledyard*.) Then Mungo Park (on his second journey), together with all his thirty-five companions and attendants—every one perished. Then Park's son, who set out in search of his father; then Harnemann, the German, in Egypt; Nicholls, on the coast of Guinea; Captain Tuckey, on the river Congo; Major Peddie and Captain Campbell; the famous Clapperton, Major Laing, Richard Lander, and a host of others, all met their death. Similar was the fate of the trading expedition, in two steamers, that followed upon Lander's discovery of the mouth of the Niger: of the crews, only four out of nineteen, in the one vessel, and five out of twenty-nine, in the other, survived. Look, too, at the

permitting the exile of Africans from their native shore—namely, that they or their descendants might return again, and become the great means of giving freedom, civilization, and Christianity to Africa itself.

And this call, we are sure, will be answered; the free men of color in the United States will at length understand the nature of the great work that lies before them—the duty they owe to themselves, to their descendants, and to their African kindred—and will engage heartily in it. Nay, this they are already doing to a considerable extent; the emigration to Liberia is now fast increasing. Accounts from New York, of the date of May 18, 1853, mention that since the beginning of that month, six vessels, carrying 800 colored emigrants, had sailed from the United States to Africa. If, in eighteen days, 800 emigrants had taken their departure, the number in a year must amount, it may be presumed, to some thousands. But this is only the beginning: emigration, we know, increases in a geometrical ratio. The emigration from Europe to America, which once was limited to a few hundreds or thousands, is going on now at the rate of nearly half a million a-year. Ireland alone sends out her hundred thousand yearly. What shall prevent the free blacks of America from emigrating, by and by, at a similar rate? Nor will these need to be transported at the expense of the Colonization Society, as was

disastrous results of the Government Expedition, in 1841. This fatality, we believe, has a deeper cause than *merely* the natural effect of climate; for Park stood the climate tolerably well. But Divine Providence is guarding Africa. He does not mean it to become another India, subject to the white man's rule, nor to be corrupted by the white man's selfishness and hardness necessarily the case with the first settlers: they will transport themselves. Many of the free blacks have means; and those who have not will be helped by those who have. How do the starving Irish contrive to emigrate in such vast numbers? Where there is a *will*, there will be found a *way*. In fact, the free blacks are emigrating now as fast, perhaps, as the young African republic can make preparations to receive them; but every company that goes will prepare the way for more, by a more extensive cultivation of the soil, and by establishing new settlements,—till by and by the flourishing and vigorous colonies will be able to receive their tens or even hundreds of thousands of immigrants yearly, both without danger on the score of support, and without detriment to the cause of liberty and order, but, on the contrary, with benefit to all parties concerned. Emigration on such a scale would soon exhaust the numbers of the free blacks in America—would soon remove them all; for, as before said, they are but between four and five hundred thousand altogether.

We will conclude this part of our subject by quoting the following eloquent passage from Mr. Freeman's *Plea*, describing the present condition of the free blacks in the United States, and presenting, at the same time, a well written memorial adopted by the people of color themselves at a meeting held some years since in the Bethel and African churches in the city of Baltimore:—

" Look at their unwelcome reception, wherever they go, among the whites; and consider the fact that their presence is regarded as an evil wherever they are. To some States they are prevented from going, by enactments which expose them to a forfeiture of their freedom, if they should dare set foot upon the soil. Louisiana, sometime since, required all free persons of color who had removed to the State since the year 1825 to leave it. Thousands, who had taken refuge in Ohio, driven out from that State, sought a home in Canada; but the result is, that the Canadians, in their turn, have threatened their expulsion. They are laid under restrictions which cannot but be exceedingly painful, in most of the States both North and South; and in none do they enjoy anything much better than a nominal freedom. Various expedients are resorted to by the State Legislatures, to deliver themselves from a free colored population, by disabilities and other embarrassments. The South casts them off; the North has no place for them; the West pushes them away; Canada threatens to expel them: and where shall they go?—what shall they do? They are here isolated; they have no home of their own, no community of their own, no country of their own, no government of their own,—no system whatever, intellectual or moral, in which their individual existence forms a part of the machinery; but every cheerful hope seems crushed. They are, I was going to say, dislocated from humanity. —The free people of color in Baltimore seem to have taken a correct though painful view of this subject, in a memorial which is now before me. Addressing the citizens of Baltimore, they thus speak:

"'We have hitherto beheld, in silence, but with intense interest, the efforts of the wise and philanthropic in our behalf. If it became us to be silent, it became us also to feel the liveliest anxiety and gratitude.

The time has now come, as we believe, in which your work and our happiness may be promoted by the expression of our opinions. We reside among you, and yet are strangers; natives, and yet not citizens; surrounded by the freest people and most republican institutions in the world, and yet enjoying none of the immunities of freedom. This singularity in our condition has not failed to strike us as well as you; but we know it is irremediable here. Our difference of color, the servitude of many and most of our brethren, and the prejudices which those circumstances have naturally occasioned, will not allow us to hope, even if we could desire, to mingle with you, one day, in the benefits of citizenship. As long as we remain among you, we must be content to be a distinct caste, exposed to the indignities and dangers, physical and moral, to which our situation makes us liable. All that we may expect is, to merit, by our peaceable and orderly behavior, your consideration and the protection of your laws. It is not to be imputed to you that we are here. Your ancestors remonstrated against the introduction of the first of our race who were brought amongst you; and it was the mother-country that insisted on their admission, that her colonies and she might profit, as she thought, by their compulsory labor. Leaving out all considerations of generosity, humanity, and benevolence, you have the strongest reasons to favor and facilitate the withdrawal from among you of such as wish to remove.

"'But if *you* have every reason to wish for our removal,—how much greater are *our* inducements to remove! Though we are not slaves, yet we are not free. Beyond a mere subsistence, and the impulse of religion, there is nothing to arouse us to the exercise of our faculties, or excite us to the attainment of eminence. Though, under the shield of your laws, we are partially protected, not oppressed—nevertheless, our situation will and must inevitably have the effect of crushing, not developing the capacities that God has given us. We are, besides, of the opinion, that our absence will, by the permission of Providence, *accelerate the liberation* of such of our brethren as are in bondage. When such of us as wish and may be able, shall have gone before to open and lead the way, a channel will be left, through which may be poured such as hereafter receive their freedom from the kindness or interest of their masters, or by public opinion and legislative enactment, or who are willing to join us who have preceded them.

"'Of the many schemes that have been proposed, we must approve of that of African Colonization. If we were able and at liberty to go whithersoever we would, the greater number, willing to leave this community, would prefer Liberia on the coast of Africa. We shall carry your language, your customs, your opinions, and Christianity, to that now desolate shore, and thence they will gradually spread with our growth far into the Continent. The slave-trade, both external and internal, can be abolished only by settlements on the coast. We foresee that difficulties and dangers await those who emigrate, such as every infant establishment must encounter and endure. But "Ethiopia shall yet lift up her hands unto God." Thousands and tens of thousands, poorer than we, annually emigrate from Europe to your country, and soon have it in their power to hasten the arrival of those they left behind. If we were doubtful of your good-will and benevolent intentions, we would remind you of the time when you were in a situation similar to ours, and when your forefathers were driven by religious persecution to a distant and inhospitable shore. An *empire* may be the result of our emigration, as of theirs.' "*

* Freeman's *Plea for Africa*, Conversation XVIII.

SECTION VI.

SLAVERY IN AMERICA—ITS ORIGIN—AND THE PROBABLE MANNER OF ITS REMOVAL.

THE subject of slavery in the United States has been too often spoken of in the language of mere feeling—nay, it may be said, of passion. Writers and speakers, uninformed, many of them, alike as to its origin and its real present condition, have indulged themselves in violent denunciations, such as could possibly serve no good purpose, but which rather tended to exasperate the master, and consequently to rivet more firmly the shackles of the slave. Zeal without knowledge, feeling without understanding, ever defeat their own ends. Mere passion is blind; and dashing recklessly forwards, it more commonly rushes to its own destruction, than accomplishes that of its adversary. What is our purpose? Is it to pour forth declamation? or is it to effect a useful end,—to do real and practical good? It is easy enough to denounce any evil: the light of absolute truth held up to evil shows clearly its deformity; and when we have ourselves no part in it, it is very easy and very natural to get up an excitement of feeling, and a ready outcry against it. But is it strictly just, it may be asked, to look at any evils of our fellow-men in this way? Could we bear to have the same bright light of abstract truth turned upon us? Have we no evils and sins of our own, which, if the Divine justice were to call us to account for, as rigorously as we are ready to call our fellow-men to account for theirs, would bring down fearful condemnation on our heads? "Cast first the beam out of thine own eye," said the Savior, "and then shalt thou see clearly to cast out the mote from thy brother's eye." It is well that we have a more lenient as well as a wiser Judge of our actions, than weak man, or we should all fare hardly enough. Happily, there is One, who knows all the palliating circumstances connected with our disordered condition; who knows how we came into it in the first place—sometimes through no fault of our own; and who knows, furthermore, what efforts we have used against the evil, and who has seen us, perchance, though often falling, yet rising again and striving to do better. Our All-wise Judge can alone be perfectly just, as well as good, because He alone knows and can make allowance for all our weaknesses, our unavoidable errors, the defective nature of the instruments we have to work with, and the difficulty of the task to be accomplished. Whereas harsh and ignorant man looks only at the general appearance, the mere surface of things; and if that looks wrong, he is ready, forgetting his own sins, to pronounce upon it a sweeping condemnation. This is neither mercy nor justice; and it was in view of this uncharitable tendency on the part of man, that the Divine Savior gave the command, "Judge not, that ye be not judged."

In order to form an opinion with any degree of justness concerning slavery in Ameri..., we must not only be possessed of true and accurate information as to its actual condition, but we must also recur to its origin and history, inquire how it came there; that thus a just share of the blame, if blame there be, may be laid upon its originators, and not the whole of it be thrown—as by the unreflecting multitude it is too apt to be done—on those who happen to have been born where it exists. Now, looking at the subject from this last point of view, it may justly be said, that slavery is the *misfortune* rather than the *fault* of America. It is owing mainly to her *situation*, as a part of the New or Western World, that she has slavery, and England not. Had England been situated where Virginia or where Cuba is,—in the New, instead of in the Old World,—would not England be as full of African slaves at this moment as they are? Was it not Englishmen who in great part supplied America with the slaves she has—English ships, with English crews, sailing from English ports, sent forth by English owners, under the full approval of the English Government?* In the year 1786, England had engaged in the slave-trade no fewer than 130 vessels (and this was full fourteen years after the English courts had declared

* The first slaves were brought into Virginia by a Dutch ship, in 1620; but after that date the English had nearly a monopoly of the traffic. So late as 1807, Dr. Chalmers, then a young man, witnessed the departure of a slave-ship from Liverpool, on her voyage to Africa, when "the ladies," he says, "waved their handkerchiefs from the shore, to sanctify what was infamous, and deck the splendid villainy of the trade."—See Hanna's *Life of Chalmers*, vol. i., ch. 5.

that no slave could be held in England itself). In 1713, she made a treaty with Spain to supply the Spanish colonies, in thirty years, with 144,000 slaves.† Now, had England been situated on the American continent or coast, would not these English ships have brought the slaves *home*, into their own territory, as the Cubans now do into theirs?—and thus would not England have been filled with African slaves, just as Cuba or the United States now are? Where, then, would have been the boast concerning the free English soil?"‡ We may thus see that the fact of Britain's

† Freeman's *Plea for Africa*, Conversation XI.—In like manner, the *French* Guinea Company, in the year 1702, contracted to supply the Spanish West Indies, in ten years, with 38,000 negroes. In truth, all, or nearly all the nations of Europe, English, French, Italians, Dutch, Danes, Spanish, Portuguese, have been concerned more or less, in the African slave-trade. None of them, then, can with justice cast reproaches on America; for if she has been guilty of receiving the stolen goods, they have been guilty of the still greater crime of *taking* them.

‡ "When England," remarks Mr. Freeman, "introduced slavery into her American colonies, she had as much free labor at home as the landholders wished to employ; and it has been on this account, and this only, that the poet was enabled to say,

'Slaves cannot breathe in England; if their lungs
Receive our air, that moment they are free;
They touch our country, and their shackles fall.'

"The fact is, that respiration could go on well enough in those parts of her dominions where free labor was not to be obtained. In America was a widely extended territory, with a soil and climate adapted to the raising of the most profitable articles of commerce. In order to render the colonies an immediate and productive source of revenue, which was the settled policy of England, and on which she placed great reliance,— an immediate supply of labor was necessary. As an expedient to provide for her colonial wants, she commenced filling her colonies with African slaves. She would not tolerate slavery at home, and yet would provide for and establish the evil among her distant children.—How being now free, while a portion of America is unhappily under the curse of slavery, is owing to nothing what-

inappropriate, then, the praise bestowed by Cowper on his native country, in the lines which follow those just quoted:

'That's noble and bespeaks a nation proud
And jealous of the blessing.'"

Plea, Conversation VII.

In view of these facts, too, any taunts or reproaches against America on the subject of slavery,—as Mr. Freeman justly remarks, "come with a peculiarly *ill grace*" from England.

We occasionally see in English journals, and in the books of British travelers in America, extracts from Southern newspapers, containing advertisements for the recovery of runaway slaves; and these are commented on in terms of astonishment and indignation. But let such writers peruse the following advertisements, selected from old English newspapers, published while slavery existed in England itself:—

"A black boy, about 15 years of age, named John White, ran away from Colonel Kirke, the 15th inst.; he has a silver *collar* about his neck, upon which is the Colonel's coat of arms and cypher; he has upon his throat a great scar. Whosoever brings the aforesaid boy to Colonel Kirke's house near the Privy Garden, will be rewarded.—*London Gazette*, March, 1665."

"To be sold, a negro boy, about 14 years old, warranted free from any distemper, and has had those fatal to that color; has been used two years to all kinds of household work, and to wait at table; his *price* is £25, and would not be sold, but the person he belongs to is leaving off business. Apply to the bar of the George Coffee House in Chancery Lane, over against the gate.—*London Advertiser*, 1756."

These advertisements may be seen, re-published, as curiosities, in the *Glasgow Herald* of Sept. 17, 1856.

It was not till 1772 (just three years before the commencement of the American Revolutionary War) that, by a decision of the Court of King's Bench, the sale of a negro in England was declared illegal. Now, Cowper's *Task*, in which is contained the often quoted British boast that "no slave can breathe in England, &c." was published in 1788, and thus was founded on a condition of things which had existed but thirteen years, and which had been brought about, not by any marked revolution in public opinion, nor established by any deliberate decision of the British Parliament, but simply by the construction of a court of law.

ever other than the difference of *local situation*—and not in any degree ascribable to any superiority in the character of the inhabitants! Then, what ground, in truth, is there for boasting? Few think of these things —because, as before observed, the multitude do not reflect; in fact, they do not *know* the history or origin of things; they look merely at the present appearance, and acquit or condemn accordingly. But the educated and the just-minded should look more thoroughly and judge more justly!

But it may be said, perhaps, that England has exculpated herself by emancipating her own slaves, and that therefore she may justly call upon America to emancipate hers, or may justifiably reproach her for continuing a course of wrong which she herself has given up. But, pause a moment! Are the two cases at all parallel? Is it true that England has done what she calls upon America to do? By no means: the cases are altogether different. England had no slaves to give up—England had no deep-rooted institution of slavery within her own borders, as America has. What England has done, in fact, is simply this —to exercise a power which she happened to possess over certain *other* countries, and to take away slavery from *them*. For the West India Colonies, though nominally or politically belonging to her, and hence under her power—nevertheless, as far as the institution of slavery was concerned, stood in the relation to her of distant and foreign countries, with whom, though she had a political connection, she had very little more social sympathy than with the United States themselves. So that she could, afar off, coolly look at the evil of slavery existing in those colonies, pronounce it wrong, and, having the power, could and did proceed to remove it. In this she had scarcely more sacrifice to make than she would have in seeing it removed from the United States, or any other part of America. The twenty millions which she undertook to pay by way of remuneration, was indeed, so far, a sacrifice,—but it was a sacrifice trifling indeed, and scarcely felt at all, compared with that which would be required of a country removing slavery *from itself;* for in that case, not only would it be necessary to make a far greater pecuniary sacrifice, but that would be the least part of it: the grand difficulty lies in giving up old habits, changing long-rooted institutions, completely inverting a long-established social order,—all of which things, we know, it is most difficult for men to do. Had the English Colonies themselves—or had the English slave-owners in those Colonies—voluntarily given up their slaves, that would indeed have been in some measure a parallel case with what is required of America: or had Great Britain possessed the institution of slavery on her own soil, in London and Yorkshire, in Edinburgh and Glasgow, and then had shown the magnanimity and moral courage to pass an act of Parliament, uprooting at once that old institution, and, contrary to all long-cherished customs, feelings, and social habits, had given up and set free at once three millions of slaves—that would indeed have been a parallel case to America's. But is there any likelihood that this would have been done? When Great Britain finds it so hard to make even trivial changes in her own long-established institutions, deep-rooted usages and customs,—is there the least probability that she would have been able, all at once, to make so vital and radical a change as this? If not, then she should be sparing of her reproaches against America, for this is just her difficulty.*

But, in truth, moreover, due credit has never been given to America for the serious and, to a considerable extent, successful efforts which she has already made to rid herself of this evil. Very early, and while yet in her colonial state, did she, from her own religious sense of justice, make these efforts—taking the lead, in fact, of all the world in this respect. In the first place, she opposed at the outset the introduction of the slaves whom the mother-country for her own selfish ends would thrust upon her, and she strove by various means to stop or check the infamous trade. The

---

* The following remarks on this head from a London journal contain, we think, much truth:

"Can we forget our own position? It is scarcely different from that of a newly reformed drunkard, remonstrating with a youth whom he himself has corrupted,—*England forced slavery upon America.* Her statesmen plotted, her diplomatists bargained, and her armies fought, to secure the detestable monopoly of supplying the New World with negroes. —From the guilt of slavery itself, how long have we been free? scarce fifteen years. And how was that guilt removed? Only by the indomitable perseverance of a few nobler spirits, who, in despite of neglect and odium, gradually worked up the nation to the great measure of abolition. —If, instead of having 800,000 slaves, we, like America, had four times that number; if, instead of being confined to distant dependencies, we had the institution interlaced with all our social arrangements at home; if, instead of being able to buy off the evil with a sacrifice which was almost imperceptible,—we had, with less resources, to incur a far mightier cost; and if we saw or believed that even the agitation of the subject was jeopardizing a Constitution which stood between us and anarchy, who will be bold enough to say, that we should, even at the present time, have cleared ourselves wholly from the crime?"—London *Inquirer*, June, 1851.

Colony of Virginia, for instance, passed no less than *twenty-three* acts, tending to suppress this traffic—all of which acts were negatived by the English Government.* In 1772, before the Declaration of Independence, the Assembly of Virginia went so far as to set forth, in a respectful petition to the king, the inhumanity of the slave-trade, and to suggest that "it might endanger the very existence of his American dominions." And to show her sincerity—in 1778, as soon as she got the power into her own hands—in the very midst of the war of independence—the same Colony passed an act making the slave-trade punishable by death.† This was nearly thirty years before the slave-trade was abolished in Great Britain. Other Colonies followed the example of Virginia in the effort to exclude or check the introduction of slaves. New York laid a duty upon their importation as early as 1753, Pennsylvania in 1762, and New Jersey in 1769.

The United States, as a nation, also, was the first to prohibit the prosecution of the slave-trade. In the year 1794—thirteen years before any act on the subject was passed by Great Britain—it was enacted by the Congress of the United States, that "no person in the United States should fit out any vessel there, for the purpose of carrying on any traffic in slaves." In 1800, it was enacted that "it should be unlawful for any citizen of the United States to have any property in any vessel employed in transporting slaves from one foreign country to another, or to serve on board any vessel so employed;" and any of the commissioned

---

* Freeman's *Plea*, Conversation XIII. See also Walsh's *Appeal*, sect. ix. † Ibid.

vessels of the United States were authorized to seize and take any American vessel found engaged in the slave-trade. In 1807, it was enacted, that after the first of January, 1808, "it should not be lawful for any one (whether American or foreigner) to bring into the United States or the territories thereof, any negro, mulatto, or person of color, with intent to hold or sell him as a slave;" and heavy penalties were imposed on the violators of this or the other acts of similar import. This was the very year in which, after twenty years' struggle, the act was passed by the British parliament for the abolition of the slave-trade. Thus the American and British acts, completely abolishing the African slave-trade, date from precisely the same period,— though in her two previous acts for its partial abolition (that is, abolition as far as her own citizens were concerned), America has the precedence.* Finally, in 1820, the American Congress passed an act, declaring that any citizen of the United States found engaged in the slave-trade should be adjudged a *pirate*, and on conviction should suffer *death*. A similar act was not passed in Great Britain till 1824: here, again, America had the precedence and set the example.†

* It thus appears, that no slaves have been allowed to be introduced into the United States for nearly half a century; and yet some British writers and speakers on this subject are so ill informed as to suppose that the foreign slave-trade is still actively carried on there. How can they expect to address American slave-owners with effect, while thus ignorant of the simplest facts of the case?

† "In 1805," says the distinguished Professor Silliman, "I went on board of a new slave-ship in Liverpool. It was just finished, and had not then been employed. I went below deck, and examined the narrow cells and the chains, which were as yet unstained with blood, but they

K

Do not these facts prove a sincere purpose and earnest endeavor, on the part of Americans, both in their Colonial and in their National capacities, to do all in their power to put a check to the evil, and stop the further progress of a wrong, the commencement of which it was not in their power to prevent?

But the question is often asked, why does not the Government of the United States abolish slavery itself, as well as forbid the slave-*trade?* To this it is to be replied, that the American Government has no power to do so: the Congress of the United States has no power whatever over slavery within the limits of the different States. It should be understood that the United States is a Confederacy, composed at present of thirty-three different States, each of which is sovereign and independent as to all its internal concerns. To understand this—it is to be remembered that before the War of Independence there were thirteen distinct Colonies, entirely independent of, and unconnected

were all ready for the victims, which, no doubt, were found and transported from Africa into slavery in that very ship. Our English friends, when they taunt us Americans on the subject, should remember that they forced slavery upon us, when we were their colonies. George III., in 1774, disallowed an act of the legislature of Virginia, prohibiting the slave-trade, because he said it would be very injurious to the commerce of his Majesty's subjects. The reformation is rather too recent to justify recrimination on the child."—*Visit to Europe in* 1851.

So late as 1807, Dr. Chalmers (as already mentioned) witnessed the departure of a slave-ship from Liverpool to Africa—when "the ladies," he says, "*waved their handkerchiefs* from the shore, to sanctify what was infamous, and deck the splendid villainy of the trade."—See Hanna's *Life of Chalmers*, vol. i., chap. 5.

So slow, in England, was the growth of right public sentiment on this subject! Long before this the Americans had abolished the slave-trade, so far as their own ships were concerned.

with, each other, yet all subject to the mother country, Great Britain. Each Colony had its own government, its governor, and its House of Assembly,—very much as Canada now has—by which all its internal affairs were regulated, subject, however, to the veto of the Government at home. At the commencement of the War of Independence, the thirteen Colonies united in a league or Confederacy, for purposes of mutual aid and defence. They appointed a general body, called a *Congress*, composed of representatives from the different Colonies, to regulate the general concerns of the Confederacy, each Colony, however, reserving to itself the management of its own internal affairs, as before. After their independence was attained, the present Constitution of the United States was adopted, in 1789, which retains still nearly all the general features of the original Confederacy. The Congress, composed like the British Parliament of an upper and a lower house, called a *Senate* and a *House of Representatives*, has power over matters of a general or national character, such as questions of peace and war, intercourse with foreign nations, regulation of import duties, and so forth; but it is provided, in the Constitution, that each State shall have the exclusive regulation of all its internal concerns, precisely as in former Colonial times: over these, therefore, the national Congress has no control whatever. Each State has its own Legislative Assembly, which enacts all laws and regulates all matters within its own confines.

Now, some of the States have slavery existing within their borders, and some have not. At present a majority of the States, namely eighteen out of the thirty-three are Free States; in these, slavery has either been abolished or has never existed: the other fifteen are Slave-holding States. Moreover, as appears by the census of 1850,—in the Free States the population is *thirteen* millions and upwards, whereas the white population in the Slave States is but little more than *six* millions. Thus it appears that less than one-third of American citizens are slave-owners, or even dwellers in the States where slavery exists. Is it right, then, to stigmatize the whole nation for the doings or for the condition of a small minority ?—to cast upon all Americans a reproach which, at worst, belongs to less than one-third of their number, and which even with those, as already shown, may be justly considered rather their misfortune than their fault, since it was imposed upon them by others ?*

But, to the citizens of the Free States, not only is the negative credit due, of being free from the

---

* Much denunciation has been uttered on the subject of the " Fugitive slave law " (as it is called), by persons who are probably ignorant of the real grounds on which that act was passed. The greatest reluctance was felt and expressed by many of the representatives from the Free States, to pass any Act by which fugitives should be returned to bondage, but there was no escaping from it but by the violation of their oath. In the original compact between the States,—called the " Constitution of the United States " (which every public officer is sworn faithfully to maintain), there is the following provision (Article iv., Section 2): " No person held to service or labor in one State, under the laws thereof, *escaping into another*, shall, in consequence of any law or regulation therein, be discharged from such service or labor; but shall be delivered up on claim of the party to whom such service or labor may be due." Thus the law already existed; for the Constitution is the supreme law of the land. The Act, above referred to, was simply a law to carry into execution this provision of the Constitution.

reproach of slavery, but to many of those States great positive praise is due, for having actually, at a great sacrifice, *abolished* slavery within their respective limits. Hardly had the yoke of subjection to Great Britain been thrown off, when the Northern States set themselves earnestly and conscientiously to this task (for, through the influence of the mother country, slaves existed, it is to be remembered, in all the Colonies, even in Massachusetts and in the city of Boston). As early as the year 1780, in the very midst of the War of Independence, the State of Pennsylvania, one of the largest and most populous of the States, set the example, by passing an Act for the gradual abolition of slavery within her boundaries. "This has the merit," says Mr. Freeman, of being the earliest legislative proceeding of the kind in any country."* This noble example was followed, at different periods, by all the other States to the north and east of Pennsylvania, namely, New York, New Jersey, New Hampshire, Massachusetts, Connecticut, and Rhode Island. Thus, *seven* of the original thirteen States have already abolished slavery within their limits.

And the good work would doubtless have gone on, had not a most unwise system of violent attack and denunciation been commenced by a party at the North,—composed at first of a few individuals, who were determined that slavery should be put an end to at once, without considering the impossibility of such a thing, under the circumstances. "One by one,"

* *Plea for Africa*, Conversation XIII.

remarks a correspondent of the London *Times*,* "The more northern States abolished slavery—all of them by gradual emancipation—and the process was going on with healthful progress, until a faction arose, which demanded the immediate emancipation of the Southern slaves. This it was impossible to achieve, and consequently folly to demand." The effect of this unwise course, on the part of a portion of the citizens of the Free States (urged on, too, with equal inconsiderateness, by societies and public meetings in Great Britain) has been to put a dead stop, in the Slave States, to all movements in reference to the abolition of slavery. Formerly—before this violence commenced—public meetings were held from time to time in Virginia, Kentucky, and other Slave States, for the purpose of devising some means for the removal of slavery within their respective limits, and bills providing for gradual emancipation were even introduced into the Legislatures. A bill to this effect, it is understood, brought into the Legislature of Kentucky, lost its passage by only *one* vote, and in all probability would in a year or two have actually passed; but the system of violent attack and denunciation having in the meantime sprung up, the favorable movement was checked at once, and at length completely stopped. Any one who knows human nature might have predicted this result. Men were not disposed to be driven and scourged to their duty; they did not need to have such an influence brought to bear upon them, and

* Of June 21, 1853.

they would not submit to it. Abuse certainly never had the effect of softening men's hearts, nor was it ever an aid, with men of independence and self-respect, in the accomplishment of any good purpose. To give respectable individuals the appellations of "robbers" and "man-stealers" because they happened to be born in a part of the country where slavery existed, and upon plantations on which their fathers had dwelt before them, and amidst a condition of things which, though bad in itself, they had no share in producing, and saw no means at once of remedying—such language could have no possible effect but to excite feelings of indignation, and to close the ears of citizens of the South against every allusion to the subject.*

Such has been the disastrous effect of this most unwise course. And not only this,—but it has operated injuriously on the condition of the slaves themselves, by increasing the severity of the masters,—compelling them to take extraordinary precautions against insurrection, and thus depriving the negroes of many privileges they had formerly enjoyed. Thus do violence and fanaticism ever defeat their own ends:

---

* "In a certain paper," says Mr. Freeman, "the writer having selected passages from the writings of such men as Mr. Clay, Gen. Harper, President Caldwell, and others, exclaims—'*Ye crafty calculators! ye hard-hearted incorrigible sinners! ye greedy and relentless robbers! ye contemners of justice and mercy! ye trembling, pitiful, pale-faced usurpers! my soul spurns you with unspeakable disgust.*' I cannot think that good men, even among abolitionists, can approve of this language."—*Plea,* Conversation IX. No! such violence and grossness of abuse as this could never avail in any cause, and is never needed in a good cause: the spirit that could indite such a sentence was not from above.

as the Apostle affirms, "the wrath of man worketh not the righteousness of God."

It is greatly to be regretted, however, that the wiser and nobler-minded of the citizens of the South should suffer themselves to be turned from the manifest path of duty on which they had entered, by such attacks as these. The true man goes straight on in the path of right, allowing himself neither to be stopped by opposition, nor urged on faster than he sees to be wise by goading, nor turned from his course in any direction either by shouts or sneers: he keeps right on, gently but firmly, in the path that conscience marks out, trusting in his God, and sure that a blessing will at length crown his faithful efforts.

A course very different from that of the northern fanatics has been taken by the authoress of that remarkable work, *Uncle Tom's Cabin*. Instead of closing the ears and clenching the hands of the citizens of the South, by violent and bitter attacks, she has striven to touch their hearts and arouse their sympathies by a series of affecting pictures, such as we are sure will reach the feelings of thousands and tens of thousands of lofty-minded men and tender-hearted women in the slave-holding States. Anxious to be just as well as compassionate, she has evidently sought to give faithfully both sides of the picture; showing the many ameliorating circumstances in the slave-relation as it really exists, and making it a very different thing from the scene of universal wailing and lashing, in which it has appeared to the excited imaginations of many. She has presented to us a view of the truly cheerful and peaceful cabin of "Uncle Tom," in Kentucky, together with the merriment of Andy and "black Sam," and the easy and contented condition of all the people of Mr. Selby's plantation—a true specimen, doubtless, of hundreds of others. She has brought before us, too, the representative of another large class—the frank and noble-hearted St. Clare, the considerate and affectionate master, conscious of all the wrongs and evils of the system, yet seeing no distinct way of removing it. Here, too, "Uncle Tom" has a pleasant home, with the little angel Eva to light his path and point him to the skies. But then, in the next place, she sets forth—in a manner that goes to the heart—the terrible evil of the system itself, which, like a devouring monster, can break into these paradises, and seizing its victim, carry him away to be tortured to death in the den of a Legree. The authoress has treated the subject in a truly philosophical manner. It is the enormous and irremediable evils of the system as a system —of the institution as an institution—which she seeks to expose; not merely presenting scenes of suffering and cruelty, which thousands of slave-holders may justly deny having anything to do with, and which they would feel as great an abhorrence of as any,—but by the course of her story she seeks to make manifest, what none can deny, namely, that the system itself, in permitting human beings to be sold to the highest bidder, renders all at any time *liable* to the extremest cruelties, either through the insolvency or death of even the kindest master. It is the essential wrong of the system, as manifested in its *capabilities* and *possibilities*, that she seeks to bring out; and in so treating her subject, she has shown a mind able to grasp its central principle. While, at the same time, the dramatic power she has evinced in the various scenes set forth in illustration of this principle, the alternating humor and pathos with which the story is told, and above all, the truly religious and Christian spirit that vivifies and elevates the whole, make the work one of such true and sanctified genius, as justly entitles it to the world-wide admiration it has obtained.

But what distinguishes this writer from most of the former opponents of slavery, is her freedom from all bitterness, and the just and Christian spirit in which she makes allowance for the difficulties of the slaveholders' position, and for the partial insensibility to the evils of the system which education and habit naturally engender. "Some have supposed it," she says, "an absurd refinement to talk about separating principles and persons, or to admit that he who upholds a bad system can be a good man. Systems most unjust and despotic have been defended by men personally just and humane. It is a melancholy consideration, but no less true, that there is almost no absurdity and no injustice that has not, at some period of the world's history, had the advantage of some good man's virtues in its support."* The excellence of the spirit in which she writes is well represented in the following extract,—which it is to be hoped may teach

---

* *Key to Uncle Tom's Cabin*, part iv., chap. x.

a salutary lesson to many accustomed to indulge themselves in language of bitter denunciation: "This holy controversy must be one of principle, not of sectional bitterness. We must not suffer it to degenerate, in our hands, into a violent prejudice against the South; and to this end, we must keep continually before our minds the more amiable features and attractive qualities of those with whose principles we are obliged to conflict. If they say all manner of evil against us, we must reflect that we expose them to great temptation to do so, when we assail institutions to which they are bound by a thousand ties of interest and early association, and to whose evils habit has made them in a great degree insensible. The Apostle gives us this direction, in cases where we are called upon to deal with offending brethren, 'Consider thyself, lest thou also be tempted.' We may apply this to our own case, and consider that if we had been exposed to the temptations which surround our friends at the South, we might have felt, and thought, and acted as they do."*

The wise, gentle, and Christian course pursued by this writer, together with the genius and power of her work itself, will be found, we believe, to have considerable effect, in the first place, in *ameliorating* the condition of the slaves: the softening of heart which it will produce in the breasts of hundreds and thousands in the slave-holding States, will be manifested in their kinder treatment of those who are still in their hands. It is probable, also, that the able manner in which she has set forth the evils of the system will result in some

---

* *Key*, part iv., chap. x.

endeavors, on the part of the nobler-minded of the Southern people, to make a reformation in the laws of the slave-holding States on this subject. An earnest effort made in this direction would have undoubtedly great effect in lessening the pains of slavery. With only such a degree of self-denial as every man of principle may justly be called upon to make, and which every legislator should consider it his glory to manifest, laws might be passed, abolishing or greatly modifying the shameful slave-markets, checking the internal slave-trade by forbidding slaves to be brought from other States for sale, and forbidding the separation of families—as of husband from wife, or of parents from children under age. Such regulations exist even in Russia—why should they not in America? Even in Africa, *domestic* slaves, as they are called, or those born in the house, cannot be sold or very severely punished, but for some signal offence, of which they must be first convicted by a kind of public trial. Cannot some regulations be passed, putting at least a degree of restraint on the absolute will of tyrannical masters, thus tying the hands of such wretches as Legree? It is to be hoped, indeed, that there are few such; yet that they exist, every observer of human nature in any part of the world must be satisfied. Few, indeed, in the present fallen condition of humanity, can bear, without injury to themselves as well as wrong to others, to have human beings in a state of absolute subjection to their will. Such power can scarcely fail to be abused.

But, in the second place, we believe the effect of these mild yet powerful representations will be, still further, to rouse the heart and thought of the Christian men of the South, of whom there are, doubtless, hundreds of thousands,—to the question whether there be not some mode in which a system of things, so plainly wrong in itself, can be gradually removed, in a manner to be truly beneficial to all parties concerned. Where there is a will, there is a way. It is a sound theological principle, that every evil—after it is seen by the light of truth to be such—may be sooner or later removed. To think otherwise would be to make the good Creator the author or upholder of evil; for it would be to charge the Governor of the Universe with having provided no way of escape from sin and misery. But He always provides a way: man has only to seek, and he will find it. Let the noblest men of the South, then, give their minds to this task: what greater glory could there be for a legislator than to accomplish it? It must, indeed, be a slow and gradual work; for since there are fifteen different slave-holding States, all entirely independent of each other, at least fifteen different Acts must in any case be passed, before slavery could be generally abolished. But let some one State but lead the way, and others will soon be found ready to follow. Who shall it be? Which State will open this campaign against wrong? Which will have the moral courage to set this ball in motion? Kentucky, the State of Henry Clay! Will not she have the magnanimity—disregarding the denunciations of opponents—to take up the question where she left it, and pass a law ordaining that henceforth every little human being, white or black, born into existence within the limits of that State, shall be free? Such a step would raise

Kentucky high in the world's regard. Or old Virginia, " the mother of Presidents "—will she take the lead in this good work? Indeed, she has already taken the lead—or at least some of her most distinguished sons were among the first to take the initiatory steps. As early as 1777, a plan was proposed by Mr. Jefferson, in the legislature of that State, for emancipating all the slaves born after that period, educating them—the males to the age of twenty-one, and the females to that of eighteen—and establishing colonies of them in some suitable place. Let Virginia resume now this plan of her eminent citizen, and carry it into execution; and her glory will be greater than that of being " the mother of Presidents,"—she will be the mother of thousands of *men*—freemen, made such by her own act.

The example thus set by either of these would soon be followed by the two remaining border States, Maryland and Missouri, and then by others further south, Tennessee, Georgia, Louisiana, Texas. And to this course they are all urged, not only by principle, but also by manifest self-interest. *Free* labor is universally allowed to be, in the long run, far more profitable than slave labor. " That labor," says Mr. Freeman, " we should suppose most profitable, in which the laborer knows that he will derive the profits of his industry; his employment depending on his diligence, and his reward upon his assiduity. Then there is every motive to excite to exertion, and to animate to perseverance. Therefore, when the choice exists, to employ at an equal price free or slave labor, the former will be decidedly preferred, because it is regarded as more capable, more diligent, more faithful, more worthy of confidence.—'The fact is,' says one of her own distinguished citizens, 'slavery is the bane and ruin of one portion of our land, and the advantage of free labor and industry has exalted the other portion. The natural consequence is, a morbid sensibility and ever wakeful jealousy on the part of the depressed, and an increasing desire for greater gain and aggrandizement on the part of the other. Yes! it is slavery that sinks the South! See the wide-spread ruin which the avarice of our ancestral government has produced, as witnessed in a sparse population of freemen, deserted habitations, fields without culture; and, strange to tell, even the wolf, driven back long since by the approach of man, now returns, after the lapse of an hundred years, to howl over the desolations of slavery.'—The lands worn out, in a great measure under the ungrateful cultivation of slaves; the population of freemen declining, or wending their westward way; and those interests neglected which would have been cultivated by a free, white, and working population, the South feels but too sensibly every effort which other sections make to sustain themselves, as if oppressive of her,—whilst all the time, the evil, the root of evil, is slavery. The South has injured, and is crushing herself, by cherishing an evil which will yet be found to be more than can be borne. She cannot rise, while the evil remains. She *feels* it, and the other States see it to be so."*

Now, let any one of the Southern States—Virginia, Kentucky, Maryland, or any other—only pass such an Act as has been described, simply a pro-

* *Plea for Africa*, Conversation VII.

spective Act, declaring that all children born within the limits of the State after a certain day should be free—and at once she would feel new life in her veins. At once, by the simple passage of such an Act, she would step, in a manner, out of the ranks of the Slave States into those of the Free. For by so doing she changes at once her course—her line of direction: now it is retrograde,—then, it would be forward. By that step, she shows her good-will to the cause, her just purpose, her determination to pursue the right path. And just as the "prodigal" was received at once by his father with delight, simply by abandoning his sinful indulgence and turning back to his father's house;—just as the repentant sinner is beheld by angels with joy, simply for his repenting, his acknowledgment of wrong and the giving up of his evil *purpose*,—though he has not had time as yet to shake off bad habits and form good ones, —so would the passage of such an Act by any one of the slave-holding States bring down upon her the blessings and the congratulations of all good men. At once would they say,—"She has turned from the path of wrong to that of right; she has manifested a good purpose and intent; she has set out in the right direction; there is no fear of her now—all the rest is but the work of time." The States of the North could with justice utter no more denunciations against her—their lips would be closed; for this was precisely the way in which they themselves got out of the swamp of slavery; it was by prospective acts, and in this gradual manner, that they all delivered themselves from that dark incubus, and, setting out with new energies, advanced to the height of prosperity which they are now enjoying. In truth, as before remarked, by the passage of such an Act, a State would by right, pass, from the side of the Slave States to that of the Free. For, let it be observed, it is not the mere fact of having slaves within its borders, that constitutes what is called a "Slave State:" but it is such from the continuance of slavery being the fixed *policy* of the State. The moment that policy is abandoned—the moment slavery is given up as a *system*—that moment the State crosses the line, and steps upon the terra firma of Freedom. This is proved from the facts of the case. For, many years after the Northern States were termed and regarded as Free States, they still had, many or most of them, slaves within their borders. It was only so late, for instance, as the year 1846, that the State of New Jersey passed an Act liberating a considerable number of slaves that yet remained within her limits. At the census of 1840, there remained in the Free States 1,102 slaves, which number we are glad to see from the census of 1850 is now reduced to 225.* As to the border State of Delaware, which, by the census-tables for 1850, contains yet 2,289 slaves, and is there reckoned among the slave-holding States,—there seems to be a doubt, in speaking of her, whether to count her among the Slave or the Free States, though in common parlance, we believe, she is often placed among

* Indeed, there are now properly *none*, as these 225, in the State of New Jersey, are made *apprentices*, by the Act of that State to abolish slavery, passed April 18, 1846.

L

the latter. In fact, so gradually do the lines melt into each other, that the precise limits where slavery ends and freedom begins can hardly be told;—and the reason is, that when the *spirit* of slavery is broken—when the system, as such, is given up—the monster is in fact dead; the form may remain, but the malicious life is not there. In such case, the remaining bonds, as in New Jersey and Delaware, are little more than nominal.*

And this is the way, we conceive, in which slavery is to come to an end in the remaining Slave States of America,—namely, by a gradual decline, similar to

* We here append a tabular view of the number of slaves in several of what are now the Free States, for every decimal period since 1790,—showing how gradual has been the emancipation:—

	1790.	1800.	1810.	1820.	1830.	1840.	1850.
New Hampshire,	158	8	0	0	0	1	0
Rhode Island,	952	381	103	48	17	5	0
Connecticut,	2,759	951	310	97	25	17	0
New York,	21,324	20,343	15,017	10,088	75	4	0
							Apprentices
New Jersey,	11,423	12,422	10,851	7,657	2,254	674	225
Pennsylvania,	3,737	1,706	795	211	403	64	0
SLAVE-HOLDING STATES.							
Delaware,	8,887	6,153	4,177	4,509	3,292	2,605	2,290
Maryland,	103,036	105,635	111,502	107,398	102,294	89,737	90,368

In examining this table we may note that two of the slave-holding States, Delaware and Maryland (if Delaware be properly reckoned among these), are pursuing the same course as the States already free—the number of slaves in Delaware having declined from 8,887 in the year 1790, to 2,290 in the year 1850; while those of Maryland have declined from 103,036 to 90,368.

It is also to be noted as remarkable, that the number of slaves in the Free States should all have reached the figure 0 just at the year 1850—the middle of the century. By the *end* of the century, we trust that the number in many more States may have reached the same figure.

that which has taken place in the States that are now Free. The process has simply to go on as it began. No reasonable man—no one who knows anything of human nature—can entertain the expectation (however desirable it may seem) that many hundreds of thousands of slave-holders, in fifteen different States of the Union, should at once change all their ways of feeling, thinking, and doing, give up all their long-established social habits and arrangements, and sacrifice property (or what they have always been accustomed to consider as legitimate property) to the enormous amount of between two or three hundred millions sterling (a thousand or fifteen hundred millions of dollars). Such an expectation is chimerical. The case of the English West India planters is, as before shown, an entirely different one. In that case the owners did not give up their slaves at all: they were taken from them by force, and against the protestations of the proprietors, by a superior power to which they happened to be subject—namely, the British Parliament. And the latter felt themselves bound to make at least partial amends, by the payment of twenty millions sterling to the owners. But to what Power are the owners in the Slave States of America subject? To none whatever, except to themselves, or to legislatures chosen by themselves. As already explained, the general Congress has no power whatever in the matter; and the slightest attempt to interfere would be a violation of the Constitution which holds the States together, and the Union would be virtually dissolved. And in what respect would the slaves be the better off in that case? In the Union, or out of the Union, the different slave-holding States are severally supreme within their own limits. The governments or legislatures of those States are composed of slave-owners, or appointed by them. Consequently, it is most evident that emancipation, if it is ever to take place, must be a *voluntary* act on the part of the owners. Now, again, we ask, is it in human nature to expect a sudden change and revolution in all the habits, feelings, and views of the many hundreds of thousands of persons of whom the slaveholders consist? If not, then, is it not plain, that emancipation, in the very nature of the case, must be a gradual thing?*

Moreover, it is by no means certain that a sudden change in the condition of so large a population (upwards of three millions) would be productive of real and lasting benefit. All great changes, to be truly beneficial, must be gradual: it is the law of Providence; it is the law of Divine order. And a violation of that law, even with the best intentions, must always bring calamity. The course of Divine Providence is and has always been, to bear patiently with evils, removing them gently and little by little, till they can be gradually superseded by something better: whereas the

---

* "The abolition of slavery," remarks the London *Times*, "is a problem which has puzzled every American statesman since the Declaration of Independence. The manumission of American slaves, and the realization of the rights and equality of freemen, can be a work only of time. Slaves, by precipitate and ill-regulated emancipation, may be abandoned to still worse conditions of human existence, and the entire and immediate abolition of slavery might often defeat its own end. All disinterested and enlightened persons in a Free State must be enemies of slavery, but the practicability of abolition is the question."— London *Times*: Review of "Stirling's Letters from the Slave States," April 10, 1858.

course of hasty man is to pluck out an evil violently by the roots, though he leave a death-wound in its place. If Providence so dealt with us or any one of us, we should perish. But He is patient and long-suffering, gently acting upon us, here a little and there a little, removing our evils and disorderly states of mind, one by one, introducing at the same time something better in its stead, thus gradually remoulding and reforming the whole man. And just so must we do in the treatment of the body politic—society at large—which is, as it were, a collective man. We should seek to remove its disorders and purge off its humors gradually and little by little: so shall we effect a permanent cure; whereas a hasty and violent course will only lead to far greater suffering or to destruction. "A general emancipation of slaves," remarks President Porter (of the Andover Theological Institution), "to be consistent with such a regard to their good and the public good as humanity and religion demand, must plainly be the work of time. It must be accomplished by a wise system of moral influence and prospective legislation, and must allow opportunity for a preparatory change of the habits of a whole community."*

* The following letter of the late distinguished statesman, Henry Clay, sets the subject in a rational light, showing the distress which would result to numbers of the slaves themselves, from a sudden change in their condition. It was addressed to several political friends, who wrote to him in 1844 on the subject of emancipating his slaves. They expressed their high admiration of his character, their pleasure on learning that he had given freedom to his man Charles, and their desire that he would extend the same boon to those that still remained on his hands. Mr. Clay replied as follows:—

"ASHLAND, *January* 8, 1845.

"Gentlemen,—I have perused your friendly letter in the spirit in which

But, after all, the grand difficulty in the case, is not so much that of emancipating the negroes, as of disposing it was written. I was glad that the emancipation of my servant Charles meets your approbation. A degree of publicity has been given to the fact, which I neither expected nor desired. I am not in the habit of making any parade of my domestic transactions; but since you have adverted to one of them, I will say that I had previously emancipated Charles's mother and sister, and acquiesced in his father's voluntary abandonment of my service, who lives with his wife near me. Charles continues to reside with me, and the effect of his freedom is no other than that of substituting fixed wages, which I now pay him, for the occasional allowances and gratuities which I gave him.

"You express a wish that I would emancipate the rest of my slaves. Of these, more than half are utterly incapable of supporting themselves, from infancy, old age, or helplessness. They are in families. What could they do, if I were to send them forth into the world? Such a measure would be *extremely cruel, instead of humane.* Our law, moreover, does not admit of emancipation, without security that the freed slave shall not be a public charge.

"In truth, gentlemen, the question of my emancipating the slaves yet remaining with me, involves many considerations of duty, relation, and locality, of which, without meaning any disrespect to you, I think you are hardly competent to judge. At all events, I, who alone am responsible to the world, to God, and to my own conscience, must reserve to myself the exclusive judgment.

"I firmly believe that the cause of the extinction of negro slavery, far from being advanced, has been retarded by the agitation of the subject at the North. This remark is not intended for those who, like you, are moved by benevolent impulses, and do not seek to gratify personal or political ambition.

"I am, with great respect, your friend and obedient servant,

"H. CLAY."

This letter is confirmatory of some just observations on the subject by the Rev. Mr. Freeman. He says: "There is a relation, the Southerner will tell you, between the owner of slaves, and the unhappy beings who are thrown around him, which is far more complicated and far less easily dissolved, than a mind, unacquainted with the whole subject in all its bearings, is apt to suppose—a relation growing out of the very structure of society. Go, for instance, to the slave-holder, and propose to of them after they are emancipated. This has always been the difficult point, with the reflecting: and those who study the subject thoroughly, will always be met by this difficulty. The danger of setting afloat in the community so vast a discordant element as a body of three millions of people,—and the number continually increasing,—who, in the nature of things, can never amalgamate with the general mass,—might well trouble, as it has troubled, the minds of the wisest statesmen and thinkers of America. And in the contemplation of it, they have been almost driven to despair for their country; and have felt disposed to "curse the day" when Britain, in her selfish disregard of the future and the rights of others, and in her eagerness for gain, introduced this terrible evil into her colonies. This difficulty, moreover, has been, in the minds of many,

<blockquote>
him to emancipate his slaves. He feels the evils of slavery as strongly, and perhaps, more so, than you can feel them; and who can say that he has not as much benevolence in his heart as we in ours? The laws of his State, framed according to the dictates of the best judgment of legislators, forbid emancipation, except under certain restrictions, which are deemed absolutely necessary to prevent pauperism, wretchedness, and crime, and utter ruin: and here are human beings dependent upon him for protection, and government, and support. The relation he did not voluntarily assume. He was born the legal proprietor of his slaves, as much as he was born the subject of civil government,—and it is his duty, and a duty which he cannot well avoid, to make the best provision for them in his power. Too frequently, it would be just as humane, to throw them overboard at sea, as to set them free in this country. Moreover, if he turn them out to shift for themselves, he turns out upon the community those who will in all probability become, most of them, vagabonds, paupers, felons, a pest to society. He will tell you, that as a Christian, as a patriot, as a philanthropist, as an honest man, and a humane friend of the blacks, he finds insuperable obstacles to the accomplishment of what you propose."—*Plea for Africa*, Conversation VIII.
</blockquote>

the firmest stronghold of slavery. It has been argued, and with much appearance of truth, that two distinct races have never been found to exist together for any considerable length of time, except in a state of subjection the one to the other. Put them on an equality, and they will contend with each other till one or the other is subjugated or exterminated. The following remarks on this point are from the pen of an able writer:

"But even if we were to suppose the Legislature [of a slave-holding State], and consequently a majority of the people who have chosen them,—to divest themselves of these feelings or prejudices, and venture on the great experiment [of emancipation], who can pretend to say that it would be a safe one? When, in every community, men are found splitting into parties, on points of difference often so minute as to be unintelligible to a stranger,—who can foresee how much they would be aggravated where the line of separation has been drawn by nature herself; and where sensible impressions might impart their own peculiar vividness to the feelings of party animosity? This visible difference between the two races tends now to preserve public tranquillity, operating on the minds both of master and slave, and confirms the authority of the one, and the submission of the other. The master more easily persuades himself that he is naturally superior (an opinion which the most philosophical of the citizens of the South conscientiously maintain), and the slave can be more readily brought to believe that the inferiority of which he must necessarily be conscious, is the work of nature rather than of man; and he is, on that account, more resigned to his condition. But when he is once admitted to a political equality, much of this *prestige* would soon disappear. The effects of property, education, natural talent, would soon dispel the greater part of their own sense of inferiority, without proportionally altering the opinions of the whites; and the sullen ill-will, which even now occasionally exists, would be exchanged for the more bitter and implacable animosity that arises between equals and rivals struggling for the mastery. History affords little light upon this subject; but the fierce contests between the Saracenic and Gothic races in Spain,—and yet more, between the blacks and the whites of St. Domingo, which ended only in the extermination of the weaker party,—seem to be too much in accordance with the ordinary principles of our nature, not to warn us against so fearful an experiment."*

Certainly, the present condition of the great mass of the free colored population in the United States, affords but little encouragement to the sincere friends of emancipation and of the African race. Their degraded

---

* Tucker's *Life of Jefferson*, vol. i., chap. v. "It is thought by the South, and by many at the North," remarks Mr. Freeman, "that immediate emancipation would render it necessary for the whites to exterminate the blacks, or abandon the Southern soil. The late abolition of slavery in the West India Colonies is pleaded as a refutation of this idea; but those who are best qualified to judge assert that the emancipation of the slaves upon the West India estates, is a very different thing from the immediate emancipation of two [three] millions of slaves in the Southern country; and that—without raising the question of the ultimate effect upon the whites in the West Indies—the banishment of the blacks, or the expatriation or annihilation of the whites of the South, would be the necessary consequence of immediate and universal emancipation here."—*Plea*, Conversation XVIII.

intellectual and moral condition,—which is to be ascribed in great part, no doubt, to their anomalous situation, as being neither slaves nor possessing the usual rights and prospects of freemen,—has excited in many minds a question whether the blacks, emancipated under such circumstances, are real gainers in any great degree, either as to mental improvement or physical comfort, by the change.

"The circumstance," says Mr. Freeman, "that there are so few blacks that, with their freedom, avoid poverty and vice, nobly resisting the natural tendency of their condition, has led some to suppose, that however undesirable in itself slavery may be, the blacks generally gain but little, and in most instances are great losers, by emancipation. The free blacks are, as a whole, exceedingly corrupt, depraved, and abandoned. There are, indeed, many honorable exceptions among them, and it is often a pleasure which I enjoy, of bearing testimony to these exceptions; but the vicious and degraded habits and propensities of this class are known to every man of attentive observation. It has been asserted, that of free blacks collected in our cities and large towns, a great portion are found in abodes of wretchedness and vice, and become tenants of poor-houses and prisons. As a proof of this tendency of their condition, the following striking facts, among others, have been mentioned. In the State of Massachusetts, where the colored population is small, being only one *seventy-fourth* part of the whole population,—about one *sixth* of all the convicts in the State-prison are blacks. In Connecticut one *thirty-fourth* part of the population is colored, and one *third* part of the convicts. In New-York one *thirty-fifth* part are blacks; and one *fourth* of the convicts in the City State-prison are blacks. In New Jersey the proportion is one *thirteenth* colored, and of the convicts one *third.* In Pennsylvania one *thirty-fourth* part of the population is colored; and more than one *third* part of the convicts is black. We might pursue further these illustrations of the degradation of the free blacks in the non-slave-holding States, but it is unnecessary. Suffice it to say, that as appears from these statements (which are found in the First Annual Report of the Prison Discipline Society), about *one-quarter* part of all the expense incurred by these States for the support of their prisons, is for *colored* convicts. The bill of expense in three of these States, namely, Massachusetts, Connecticut, and New York, for an average period of less than eighteen years, was 164,000 dollars, upon convicts taken from a population of only 54,000 colored persons."*

This is, indeed, a fearful picture; and almost sufficient, if considered by itself, to dishearten the friends of emancipation, and deter them from further efforts, when they are seen to be followed by such lamentable results. In the slave-holding States the condition of the free blacks is said to be still worse, if possible, inasmuch as the influences surrounding them are still more debasing. "It would be easy," says Mr. Freeman, "to multiply instances showing the rapid deterioration, generally, of slaves, as respects morality, industry, and all virtue, when set free, without the stimulus afforded by a change of locality, in which encouraging prospects of due eleva-

* *Plea for Africa*, Conversations XVII. and XVIII.

tion may be presented. We will adduce the following case. The late President Madison, in a letter to a gentleman, published just before his decease, writes as follows:— 'You express a wish to obtain information in relation to the history of the emancipated people of color in Prince Edward [County Virginia]: I presume you refer, more especially, to those emancipated by the late Richard Randolph. More than twenty-five years ago, I think, they were liberated; at which time they numbered about *one hundred*, and were settled on small parcels of land of from ten to twenty-five acres to each family. As long as the habits of industry, which they had acquired while slaves, lasted, they continued to increase in numbers, and lived in some degree of comfort. But as soon as this was lost, and most of those who had been many years in slavery either died or became old and infirm, and a new race, raised in idleness and vice, sprung up,—they began not only to be idle and vicious, but to diminish instead of increasing, and have continued to diminish in numbers very regularly every year, and that, too, without emigration; for they have, almost without exception, remained together, in the same situation as at first placed, to this day. Idleness, poverty, and dissipation are the agents which continue to diminish their numbers, and to render them wretched in the extreme, as well as a great pest and heavy tax upon the neighborhood in which they live. There is so little of industry, and so much dissipation among them, that it is impossible for the females to rear their children; and the operations of time, profligacy, and disease, more than keep pace with any increase among them. While they are a very great pest and heavy tax upon the community, it is at the same time most obvious that they themselves are infinitely the worse for the exchange from slavery to liberty,—if, indeed, their condition deserve that name.'"*

From this distressing statement, we may learn the important truth—which many in their zeal are apt to forget—that freedom alone, without the intelligence and the disposition, as well as the opportunity to use it properly,—may become rather a curse than a blessing.† And from the picture here presented, which is probably not a singular one, we may gather a very distinct view of the reason why, under Divine Providence, the state of slavery is permitted to exist, until such time as it can be removed, without producing a still greater depth of moral evil than already exists in connection with the system. The reason why tyranny and despotism are permitted in the political world—the reason why the chains of the nations are not at once broken by the Divine power—is, without doubt,

---

* *Plea*, Appendix, p. 339.

† In this connection, it may be observed, that the mere escape of a slave across the line into Canada, is apt to be considered quite a sufficient guarantee of his usefulness and happiness. The following brief statement, however, by an English clergyman, sets the matter in a different and probably truer light [he is speaking of a negro woman belonging to his parish in Canada]:—" Her husband had been a slave in the States, and had made a premature liberation of himself by crossing the boundary line. Yet he could not gain a living by his skill and labor. He was a helpless and dependent creature. I perceived the necessity of conveying useful instruction to people inured to slavery, before emancipation and the rights of freedom are bestowed. Liberty to the captive is assuredly no blessing where this has not been previously provided."—Rev. Isaac Fidler's *United States and Canada*, p. 381.

because it is seen by Omniscience that the nations are not yet prepared for freedom—that they are not yet in a state to possess liberty without abusing it—thus that there would be danger of their turning the blessing into a curse. The great truth should be ever kept in mind—and the understanding and recollection of this will afford an explanation of a thousand permissions of evils in this life—that the great end, it may be said the *single* end, which the good Creator has in view for all men, and for every individual man, is his *salvation*—that is, *his happiness in eternity*. His state and condition in *time* are made altogether subservient to this end. What matters it,—a little sickness, a little pain, or trouble of any kind for these few years, in comparison with our well-being through the thousands and millions of years, the long ages of eternity? Hence it is, that health or sickness, wealth or poverty, liberty or bondage, are respectively given or permitted to us, according as in the Divine wisdom they are seen to be conducive to this end. Poor "Uncle Tom," with his body gashed with lashes, and his soul tried to its depths,—yet turning his dying eyes to his blessed Savior, and crying, "Lord, I come," and then soaring aloft, up-borne by angels, to his eternal home,—is he not better off, infinitely,—I do not say, than his murderer, Legree—but even than one of those colored freemen, described by President Madison, sunk in sloth, profligacy, and vice? And thus it is, that the Divine Being looks at all our several states and conditions, in reference always to the eternal future.

Then, till it be seen by Infinite Wisdom, that the emancipation of the colored race can be brought about without moral injury, without producing, on the whole, even a lower state of degradation than already exists, we may be sure that, it will not, in His Divine Providence, be permitted to take place. And we may be equally sure, that just so soon as the same Divine Wisdom sees that a way can be opened for that emancipation, consistently with the best spiritual and eternal interests of both blacks and whites, their deliverance from bondage will be effected. God has not forgotten nor forsaken them: He knows what He is doing; and in His own good time He will bring His great purposes to pass.

The interesting question then arises, Is there no such way opened or opening? Is there no prospect, even in the dim distance, of that glittering gate through which the African crowds are to pass from slavery to freedom? We answer—Yes! there is. In the midst of the midnight gloom, which the pictures just presented throw over the mind,—suddenly the clouds disperse, and a star of hope gleams in the morning sky. It is LIBERIA. Across the Atlantic waste, that bright land glitters to our mental view, like a light-house guiding the tempest-tossed mariner to a haven of refuge. This is the gate of freedom, which God has opened; and it stands open wide to all who are willing to enter. There the colored man can be free, and yet moral and religious. There, free from the baneful over-shadowing of the white race, he can enjoy true liberty; there he can become a true man, with all worldly encouragements and prospects to urge him on in the path of activity and usefulness,—and Heaven beckoning in the distance. Compare the elevated condition of the citizens of Liberia with the abject state of the free blacks, scattered amongst the whites of America,—and see if the former be not the true home which God has prepared for the colored race.

Yes! this is the true gate of freedom. Compass the field of slavery often as you will, and you will find no other outlet. From Africa they came, and thither they must return, if they would find a true home and lasting happiness. The Free States of America afford no proper asylum for the emancipated slave. They are indeed fast shutting their doors against them altogether: one after another, they are passing laws forbidding the entrance of blacks into their borders—whether freeborn or emancipated. Ohio, some time ago, passed such laws of exclusion. Within a short time, the States of Illinois and Indiana have not only made similar regulations, but introduced provisions of this character into their newly revised *Constitutions*, showing that it is intended as the settled policy and purpose of those States to exclude a colored population. Delaware, which but lately revised its State Constitution, introduced a similar stringent provision, and the new State of Oregon has done the same.* Even Canada, the last

---

* The law of Illinois is very severe in its terms. It provides that "every negro or mulatto, bond or free, who shall come into the State and remain ten days, with the evident intention of residing therein, shall be deemed guilty of a high misdemeanor, and be fined fifty dollars; and if the fine is not paid forthwith, he or she is to be sold at public auction to any person who will pay the fine and costs for the shortest time; and the purchaser shall have the right to compel the negro or mulatto to work for and serve out such time. And if the offender does not leave the State within ten days from the expiration of his servitude, he or she is liable to a second prosecution, the penalty being increased to one hundred

refuge of the fugitive slave, is beginning to murmur and show symptoms of uneasiness at the rapid increase of its colored population, and seems preparing to adopt measures for its exclusion.*

Now, the laws of the slave-holding States, or of most of them, absolutely forbid emancipation, unless the slaves emancipated be at the same time removed beyond the limits of the State. But we perceive, from the

dollars; and so on, with an addition of fifty dollars to the penalty for every offence."

In regard to Indiana, a New York paper of the date of June 28, 1853, states that "the free negroes of that State are leaving it in hundreds in consequence of the rigid enforcement of the 18th Article of the New Constitution, by which all colored persons who came into that State since November 1, 1851, are required to leave it under heavy penalties."

The terms of the Delaware provision are as follows:—"That no free negro or mulatto, not now an inhabitant of the State, or who shall leave the State with an intention to change his residence, shall, after the adoption of this Constitution, settle in this State, or come into or remain within the State, more than ten days. All contracts made with any free negro or mulatto, coming into this State, contrary to the provisions of this section, shall be void; and any person who shall employ such negro or mulatto, or otherwise encourage him to remain in this State, shall be fined in a sum not less than twenty nor more than five hundred dollars." The Constitution of Oregon, just adopted, forbids the entrance of colored persons into the State, or their holding real estate therein, or even making contracts, or maintaining suits in any Court of the State.

* In a New York journal of the 7th June, 1853, we find the following statement, which is indicative of the state of feeling beginning to arise in Canada, in reference to the increase of blacks:—

"A petition has been presented to the Canadian Legislature from the Municipal Council of Kent, representing that by reason of the rapid increase of the colored population of the said County, by immigration from the United States, many evils are resulting and are likely to result to the said County, and praying for the adoption of certain measures in reference thereto."

regulations of the Free States, just described, that emancipated slaves will no longer be able to find a retreat within those States. In consequence, there appears no prospect for them but a condition of hopeless slavery.*

* Professor Stowe (husband of the authoress of "Uncle Tom's Cabin"), in showing the ineffectiveness of attempts at emancipation, unless united with *colonization*, that is, removal to Africa—states the following striking case:—

"In 1770, the Friends [Quakers] in the United States declared slavery to be inconsistent with the principles of Christianity, and prohibited it to the members of their body. The Friends of the Yearly Meeting of North Carolina, including a part of Tennessee and Virginia, amounting to many thousands, petitioned the Legislature of North Carolina for permission to emancipate their slaves. It was refused. They continued to press the subject with petition after petition for *forty years*, and with no better success. They, at length, without law, emancipated their slaves upon the soil; and what was the consequence? More than one hundred of those emancipated slaves were taken up and sold into perpetual and hopeless bondage, under the laws of the State. Emancipation on the soil was plainly impossible, in the existing state of public feeling. After various expedients, and having expended in ten years more than 20,000 dollars in procuring asylums for their slaves in the Free States, those Free States made enactments preventing this intrusion of free blacks upon them. Pennsylvania, New Jersey, and New York, were applied to in vain: the door was shut. Some years since they embarked one hundred of their liberated slaves for Pennsylvania. They were refused a landing in the State. They went over to New Jersey. The same refusal met them there. They were then left to float up and down the Delaware river, without a spot of dry land to set their feet upon, till the Colonization Society took them up, and gave them a resting place in Liberia. They [the Friends] have now five hundred slaves left whom they are anxious to liberate. And what shall they do? shall they get the laws of the State altered? They labored after that for forty years, and more than one whole generation of black men died in bondage, while their masters were striving to effectuate *immediate emancipation.* Immediate emancipation they found to be *so slow a process*, that they were obliged to resort to colonization in order that something might be done *immediately.*"—Freeman's *Plea for Africa*, Appendix, p. 346.

In this well-nigh desperate state of things, the star of Liberia once more appears amid the gloom. To the despairing she holds out hope: to the bound she offers deliverance and peace. This is the gate of freedom which God has opened, and it is vain to seek for any other. And through this gate, although so lately opened, how many have already passed to the enjoyment of liberty and prosperity! No sooner had the Colonization Society commenced its great undertaking, than the far-sighted Clarkson saw the good that would at once result to the cause so dear to his heart. "For myself," he says (to adduce once more his memorable words), "I am free to say, that of all things that have been going on in our favor since 1787, when the abolition of the slave-trade was seriously proposed, that which is going on in the United States is the most important. It surpasses everything that has yet occurred. No sooner had your colony been established on Cape Montserado, than there appeared a disposition among the owners of slaves to give them freedom voluntarily and without compensation, and allow them to be sent to the land of their fathers, so that you have many thousands redeemed, without any cost for their redemption. To me this is truly astonishing. Can this have taken place without the spirit of God."*—"Among the most promising and encouraging circumstances attending the career of this society," remarks the late benevolent Matthew Carey of Philadelphia, "are the numerous manumissions that have taken place in almost all the Slave States, on the express condition of the freed people being sent to

---

* See Freeman's *Plea*, Conversation XIX.

Liberia. These manumissions have occurred on a scale that the most sanguine friends of the cause could not have anticipated. Entire families have been blest with their freedom, from the most pure motives, a conviction of the immorality and injustice of slavery; and in most cases ample provision has been made for the expense of their passage, and in some, for their support also, in Liberia."

We will now adduce some particular instances of this generous conduct on the part of slave-owners, which will show distinctly the manner in which the simple existence of such a place of refuge as Liberia operates in favour of emancipation.

"Colonel Smith, an old Revolutionary officer of Sussex County, Virginia, ordered in his will, that all his slaves, *seventy or eighty* in number, should be emancipated; and bequeathed above 5,000 dollars, to defray the expense of transporting them to Liberia. Patsey Morris, of Louisa County, Virginia, directed by will that all her slaves, *sixteen* in number, should be emancipated, and left 500 dollars to fit them out, and defray the expense of their passage. Dr. Bradley, of Georgia, left *forty-nine* slaves free, on condition of their removal to Liberia. A gentleman in North Carolina, last year, gave freedom to all his slaves, *fourteen* in number, and provided 20 dollars each, to pay their passage to Liberia. William Fitzhugh bequeathed freedom to *all* his slaves, after a certain fixed period, and ordered that their expenses should be paid to whatsoever place they should think proper to go; and as an encouragement to them to emigrate to the American colony on the coast of Africa, "where," adds the will, "I believe that their happiness will be more permanently secured, I desire not only that the expenses of their emigration be paid, but that the sum of 50 dollars be paid to each one so emigrating, on his or her arrival in Africa." David Shriver, of Frederick County, Maryland, ordered by his will that all his slaves, *thirty* in number, should be emancipated, and that proper provision should be made for the comfortable support of the infirm and aged, and for the instruction of the young in reading, writing, and arithmetic, and in some art or trade by which they might acquire the means of support. Rev. Robert Cox, of Suffolk County, Virginia, provided by his will for the emancipation of all his slaves, upwards of *thirty*, and left several hundred dollars to pay their passage to Liberia. A lady near Charlestown, Virginia, liberated all her slaves, *ten* in number, to be sent to Liberia; and moreover purchased two, whose families were among her slaves: for the one of whom she gave three hundred and fifty dollars, and for the other four hundred and fifty. Mrs. J———, of Merry County, Virginia, and her two sons, one a clergyman and the other a physician, offered the Colonization Society *sixty* slaves, to be conveyed to Liberia. Rev. Fletcher Andrew gave freedom to *twenty*, who constituted nearly all his property, for the same purpose. Nathaniel Crenshaw, near Richmond, liberated *sixty* slaves, with a view to have them sent to Liberia. Mr. Isaac Ross, of Mississippi, an officer in the war of the Revolution, recently left all his slaves, *one hundred and seventy* in number, under the following conditions, namely, that after the death of his daughter (now a widow) the slaves who may be over twenty-one years of age shall decide whether they will remain in bondage, or go to Africa: if they determine to go to Africa, all the property is to be sold, and the proceeds, together with the proceeds of the crops till that time (12,000 or 15,000 dollars excepted) are to be expended in their transportation and comfortable settlement in the Colony of Liberia, and the establishment of an institution of learning in some part of the colony. A gentleman of Louisiana left *thirty*, to go to Liberia, and directed his executors to pay their passage, as well as an outfit of tools, implements of husbandry, provisions and clothes for one year, and to two of them he gave 500 dollars each. In Virginia, recently, one person has manumitted *twenty-three*, another *fifty*, another *sixteen*, and a fourth *twenty-five;* and many others, with similar and smaller numbers: but all were manumitted on condition of their going to Africa. In the State of Tennessee many similar examples have been given during the past year: one man liberated *twenty-three*, and another *twenty-one*, supplying them with ample funds, and also providing clothing for them, and furnishing them with suitable tools, and for paying the expense of their removal to Africa. The Legislature of that State, also, has promised the sum of ten dollars each, toward defraying the expenses of those who shall go to Liberia. Again, a Mr. Turpin, of South Carolina, some time since emancipated *all* his slaves, and gave them his estate, valued at 329,000 dollars. *Eighteen* were liberated by a Mrs. Greenfield, near Natchez, Mississippi, on the condition of their going to Africa; E. B. Randolph, of Columbus,

liberated *twenty*, on the same condition; William
Foster, Esq., *twenty-one;* another *twenty-eight;* a
gentleman in Kentucky, *sixty;* a lady in the same
State, *forty:* nearly all young—with very few exceptions, under forty years of age. The Society of
Friends, in North Carolina, had liberated, in 1835,
no less than *six hundred and fifty-two.*" * "Numerous
applications," continues Mr. Freeman, " are constantly
before the Society or its auxiliaries, for assistance in
emigrating to Africa. A large number of slaves are,
by the decision of their masters, free in prospect,
and in course of preparation for liberty; whilst others
will be free the moment they can find a passage to
Liberia."—" Within one year, it is said that more
than 2,000 slaves have been offered to the Colonization Society from five different States, with the
desire expressed on the part both of master and
slave, for a passage to Liberia." †

Now, what do we see here? Here is action; this
is *doing* something, and not merely talking, and passing resolutions at public meetings. Here is the thing
we have been long seeking for—emancipation—actually
in existence and in active operation: and this, too,
in the best possible manner,—not effected by force,
nor by imperative legislative enactment, but by
simply giving an opportunity for the consciences and
hearts of slave-holders, already touched, to put forth
their generous desires and intentions into act. Is
not this truly God's plan? Is not this truly a Divine
working? Can we not see the hand of Providence
here? " One instance," justly remarks Mr. Freeman,

* Freeman's *Plea*, Appendix, p. 341. † Ibid., p 161.

"of *bona fide* emancipation, in the midst of the slave-holding States, evidenced by self-denying exertions to place the emancipated blacks in a land where they may be truly free and blessed, will have more effect in freeing others, than a hundred auxiliaries at the North, or tens of thousands of speeches and resolves which never reach the eye or ear of a single slave-holder, or if they do, serve only to irritate, and shut up every avenue to conviction." And so it is: "God's ways are not as our ways, neither are His thoughts as our thoughts." We set out on a course of action, planned, as we believe, from benevolent motives,—and we push on, in our own strength, determined to overcome every obstacle, and by main force to break down all opposition, and to effect our object at every hazard:—and what is the result? we accomplish nothing: we find ourselves, after all our efforts, farther from the point aimed at than when we set out. And why? Because we have gone forward in our own strength, not in the Lord's strength: because both the plan, and the manner of its execution are from our own narrow and short-sighted understandings, made still narrower by our own obstinate wills. All this time—unobserved or despised by us—the Omnipotent and All-wise Providence is really effecting the same benevolent object, in His own quiet and peculiar manner, so working as, while accomplishing the end in view, to benefit all and injure none.

The truth of this may be strikingly seen in the present instance. Men—urged, doubtless, by benevolent motives—set their hearts on the abolition of slavery. And setting about it in their own strength, they rushed on, determined to accomplish their object at all risks, and without regard to consequences,—pouring forth violent words and imprecations, making wild gesticulations, and striking right and left, thinking, by these means, to knock off the poor slaves' chairs. But, alas! the effect of all this violence was found, in the end, only to rivet those chains the tighter, to make the heavy burden heavier, and in fact, actually to check the course of emancipation where it had already begun. In the meantime, an individual, or a few individuals, humble, good men, not setting out in their own strength, not satisfied that they knew all and could accomplish all, but looking up tremblingly to the Lord on high, and praying to be guided by His Wisdom and led by His hand, gently and quietly commenced an undertaking which was plainly most unobjectionable both in its end and in its proposed means; attacking nothing, assaulting no one, proposing a plan which seemed to them called-for at the time, and calculated to do great good, yet forcing no one, but leaving all free to avail themselves of its benefits or not, as they chose. The Constitution of the American Colonization Society simply proposed "to promote and execute a plan for colonizing, with their own consent, the free people of color, in Africa, or such other place as Congress shall deem expedient." That is the whole professed object: nothing is said about slaves, nothing about the slave-trade, nothing about civilizing Africa: it confined itself to a simple and obvious *duty*, that of affording the free people of color, who were seen to be in a depressed and degraded state, an opportunity to become *men*—to become truly free. All great things have small beginnings,—so had this; yet, beginning in this simple and humble way, this Society has been led on by Divine Providence to the accomplishment, already, of great deeds; and promises in the end to regenerate and bless with freedom and happiness two great Continents. Truly may we say, in the words of the distinguished Dr. Beecher,* that this is "God's Society." "I do not think," said he, in his Colonization address at Pittsburgh, "I do not think that a Society, heaven-moved as this Society was, by such wisdom as Samuel J. Mills was blessed with,—by such wisdom as he commanded into its service,—moved on by such faith and prayer, and so blessed of heaven as this has been in its past labors, and still is,—could have been born of wisdom from beneath. I would say of this Society, it is *God's Society.* In its commencement it was his; in its progress it has been his; and the station it now occupies in the midst of all the difficulties which have grown out of inexperience and the peculiar nature of the subject—as well as its success in Africa—all show it to be his."†

The same vigorous writer—Dr. Beecher—in the following striking passage, presents a comprehensive view of the whole matter which we have been laboring to set forth in these pages—namely, the reason for the Divine permission of the slave-trade and slavery, the after-return of those slaves to Africa by the process of colonization, and the final civilizing and Christianizing of that whole Continent. "There is no such thing,"

---

* Father of Mrs. Stowe.
† Freeman's *Plea*, Conversation XXVIII.

he begins by remarking, " as raising the human mind
without nationality. You must have the whole machinery of society, or you will never do it.—As to the
poor African, he never can rise without space to move
in, and motives to action. If you refuse to remove
him, you will have an equal number of paupers thrown
upon your shores, and then you must support both.
The ways of God are high and dreadful. He takes the
wickedest of men, and causes them to accomplish his
own purpose. "Their hearts think not so, neither do
they mean so;" but in their wickedness they do that
which God blesses and overrules for good. The coast
of Africa has been environed with dangers: it is
almost inaccessible to the approach of the white man;
and that whole Continent has yet to be civilized and
Christianized. And how is it to be done? God has
permitted what has come to pass. He has *suffered its
inhabitants to be brought here as slaves*—and the trans-
position has scarcely increased their miseries. God is
not in a hurry to accomplish His designs. By bringing them into a Christian land, He has prepared the
way for their being *thrown back, in a Christianized condition, on their native shore.* I believe that colonization, too, is destined to *stop the slave-trade.* Your
colonies will stand like a chain of light from point to
point, along the whole dark coast of benighted Africa;
and from the colonies will your missionaries go into the
interior, until they shall have spread *a belt of salvation*
over that benighted portion of the globe."*

* Freeman's *Plea*, Appendix, p. 337. Similar sentiments have also been
expressed by Dr. Beecher's distinguished daughter, Mrs. Stowe, putting
her thoughts into the mouth of her admirably drawn character, George

All these great purposes are now beginning to be accomplished. As wisely remarked by Dr. Beecher, God is not in haste to accomplish His designs. No!

Harris, in a letter addressed to his colored friends:—" The desire and yearning of our soul," he says, " is for an African *nationality*. I want a people that shall have a tangible, separate existence of its own, and where am I to look for it? Not in Hayti; for in Hayti they had nothing to start with: a stream cannot rise above its fountain. The race that formed the character of the Haytians was a worn out, effeminate one; and, of course, the subject race will be centuries in rising to anything. Where, then, shall I look? On the shores of Africa I see a Republic—a Republic formed of picked men, who, by energy and self-educating force, have, in many cases, raised themselves above a condition of slavery. Having gone through a preparatory stage of feebleness, this Republic has at last become an acknowledged nation on the face of the earth—acknowledged both by France and England. There it is my wish to go, and find myself a people.

" I am aware, now, that I shall have you all against me. But before you strike, hear me. During my stay in France, I have followed up, with intense interest, the history of my people in America. I have noted the struggle between Abolitionist and Colonizationist, and have received some impressions, as a distant spectator, which could never have occurred to me as a participator. I grant that this Liberia may have subserved all sorts of purposes, by being played off, in the hands of our oppressors, against us. Doubtless the scheme may have been used, in unjustifiable ways, as a means of retarding our emancipation. But the question to me is—Is there not a God above all man's schemes? May He not have overruled their designs, and founded for us a nation by them? In these days a nation is born in a day. A nation starts now, with all the great problems of republican life and civilization wrought out to its hand; it has not to discover, but only to apply. Let us, then, all take hold together with all our might, and see what we can do with this new enterprise; and the whole splendid continent of Africa opens before us and our children. *Our nation* shall roll the tide of civilization and Christianity along its shores, and plant there mighty republics, that, growing with the rapidity of tropical vegetation, shall be for all coming ages."— *Uncle Tom's Cabin*, chap. xliii.

These wishes seem to be now undergoing their accomplishment. A Cincinnati paper, of July 11, 1860, says: " The Africans of the United

He, who foresees all things is never in haste; for He prepares all the means in due time, and in the exact time best to accomplish the end. Just as fast as will be for the good of all concerned, for whites and for blacks, for America and for Africa, will the slaves be released and the free blacks be removed. We may aid in this cause if we will, but we cannot stop it. The ball is already in motion, and will roll on. God is pushing it, and guiding it, too: those who seek to check it, will be only crushed beneath it. But why should any wish to check it? It harms none: it moves on only to bless. No thinking man—if he will lay aside prejudice—but must see that it is better for the colored race to separate from the whites, and go to a land where they can stand upon their own feet, in true dignity and independence. No Christian and conscientious man, but will admit, that in the long run it will be best both for blacks and whites, that slavery should cease, and that nothing but freedom, joined with light and religion, should exist upon the earth. And finally, no benevolent man and lover of his kind, but must wish to see Africa elevated in the scale of nations, its chains broken, its ignorance dispelled, and the blessings of civilization and true religion spread over it from shore to shore. Then, let all unite in this great enterprise. Laying aside the language of attack and reproach on the one side, and refraining from threat and

States are beginning to see the importance of Liberia, and are moving towards that point. They are inaugurating societies among themselves to promote emigration. The Colonization Society reports that they never before had so many applications for passage to the Coast of Africa, and that more emigrants will sail this year than within the last five years."

retort on the other, let Americans of the North and of the South unite in this holy cause. While the North employs its exertions in helping off the colored population within its own borders, and aiding them to emigrate to the home of their fathers, where alone they can be truly free—the South, while performing the same service to the free blacks there, should also be left to deliberate in freedom, and without undue interference from the North, on the best means of emancipating the slave, and of preparing him, at the same time, for that freedom which every one, surely, who loves his neighbor as himself, would wish him to enjoy. And, depend upon it, there are pure consciences and warm hearts enough at the South to undertake this high enterprise, if we will but leave them to themselves. The instances already given of the numbers who have shown themselves ready to emancipate, the moment they could see the way opened,—is proof enough of this. And such emancipation, like " mercy,' will be " twice blessed :" it will benefit alike the freer and the freed. Individuals will take the first steps in the cause—and the noblest minded will be foremost. As the great Webster gave to the nation the motto— " Liberty *and* Union one and inseparable," so the motto of the friend of Liberty will be " Emancipation *and* Colonization." As the cause moves on, communities and States will take it up. Already Maryland, Mississippi, Louisiana, and other States have their own colonies on the African shores. More and more colonies will be formed, lining the whole coast, and extirpating the slave-trade for ever. State-treasuries will be opened in aid of the good work; and at length, perhaps, with general consent, the national aid will be given. Already a line of steam-ships to Africa has been proposed. America will come up as one man to the work:—and what good purpose can they not accomplish, when to it they give their hands and hearts?—till, at length, where, some years since, a few scores or hundreds only of the colored population were seen creeping over to Africa,—a whole fleet will be on its rejoicing way across the sea, carrying thousands and tens of thousands yearly on their return to their free and happy home.* Thus, all shall be freed; and both Continents shall be, in the eloquent words of the Irish orator, "redeemed, regenerated, and disenthralled, by the irresistible genius of universal emancipation."

* It is estimated that in ten years, from 1848 to 1858, upwards of *four miillons* of persons emigrated from Europe to America Now, this is a greater number than the whole colored population of the United States,—showing, thus, that their removal is a thing in itself entirely practicable.

www.ingramcontent.com/pod-product-compliance
Lightning Source LLC
Chambersburg PA
CBHW031443160426
43195CB00010BB/826